D0264362

BLITZKRIEG

RUSSIA

1942 – 1943

BLITZKRIEG
RUSSIA
1942 – 1943
WILL FOWLER

Ian Allan
PUBLISHING

First published 2003

ISBN 0 7110 2947 4

All rights reserved. No part of this book may be
reproduced or transmitted in any form or by any
means, electronic or mechanical, including photo-
copying, recording or by any information storage
and retrieval system, without permission from the
Publisher in writing.

© Will Fowler 2003

Published by Ian Allan Publishing
an imprint of Ian Allan Publishing Ltd, Hersham,
Surrey KT12 4RG.

Printed by Ian Allan Printing Ltd, Hersham,
Surrey KT12 4RG.

Code: 0310/A2

Illustrations by Mike Rose
Maps by Sue Casebourne

Picture Credits
All photographs are from Bugle Archives.

COVER PICTURE: The awesome bulk of a PzKpfw VI
Tiger 1, a tank with formidable armament and
thick armour.

PREVIOUS PAGE: PzKpfw III Ausf J tanks armed with
the long-barrelled 5cm gun deploy in loose
formation across the steppe.

Blitzkrieg: Fast armoured and mechanised
warfare supported by bombers and ground
attack aircraft.

CONTENTS

A CITY ON THE VOLGA

The drive across the Ukraine and into
the Caucasus took the German Army
in the Soviet Union to what would be the
limits of the Third Reich. On maps of
Europe it looked like a spectacular
triumph, but it held the seeds of the
ultimate destruction of Hitler's Germany.

DER TOTALER KRIEG
30-49

Stalingrad obsessed Hitler and consumed the 6th Army. Trapped within the ruins of the city the firepower and mobility of German tanks was nullified. The Soviet counter attack to north and south pulverised the poorly trained and equipped Hungarian, Rumanian and Italian troops who were holding the vulnerable flanks.

KHARKOV ARMOURED ANVIL
50-69

Manstein may have failed to lift the siege of Stalingrad, but his masterly battles of manoeuvre halted the Soviet 1943 winter offensive around Kharkov. As the front lines stabilised the huge Kursk salient was formed. This seemed the likely objective for a German summer offensive confirmed by Enigma intercepts.

UNTERNEHMEN ZITADELLE
70-94

The massive armoured battles fought to the north and south of Kursk consumed men, tanks, guns and aircraft. In the noise, smoke, fire and dust the last chances for Nazi Germany to achieve a victory that might delay or prevent defeat were consumed in a man-made inferno.

A CITY ON THE VOLGA

The struggle for Stalingrad is nearing a successful conclusion. Today or tomorrow we may expect to receive important OKW announcements about the success achieved. The German Press will have to prepare an impressive tribute to celebrate the victorious outcome of this all-important battle for the city of Stalingrad.

Daily Keynote from Reich Press Chief
Tuesday September 15, 1942

Moscow had been saved. The Soviet counter attack that pushed back the German Army Group Centre in 1941-1942 finally ground to a halt in the mud of early spring 1942. It had saved the city and made General Zhukov who had commanded the West Theatre, composed of the Kalinin, West and Bryansk Fronts, a national hero.

The ability of the German Army to recover and reform after defeats or withdrawals would, however, amaze both the Russians and the Western Allies.

On May 8, 1942 the re-armed and equipped German forces launched their new offensive *Unternehmen Blau* – Operation Blue. In savage fighting at Kharkov between May 12 and 28 they defeated a Soviet offensive by General Malinovsky's South Front, part of Marshal Timoshenko's South West Theatre, and then launched *Unternehmen Fredericus 1*

ABOVE: A British Valentine tank, shipped in an Arctic convoy, abandoned near Kharkov.

ABOVE: A ZIS-5V truck among the litter of bodies and equipment near a crossing on the Donets following Timoshenko's disastrous offensive.

LEFT: A young German NCO scans the distant horizon. The vast distances overawed men who were familiar with the streets of German cities.

against the Isyum salient and rolled eastwards. The action at Kharkov cost the Germans 20,000 men, but the Soviet losses were staggering – 214,000 men, 1,200 tanks and 2,000 guns captured in a huge pocket.

On June 1 Hitler flew to the HQ of Army Group South at Poltava to discuss attacks to the south and east. In Berlin Dr Joseph Goebbels, the *Reichsminister für Volkserklärung und Propaganda* (Reich Minister for Public Enlightenment and Propaganda), hinted to the foreign press that Moscow would be the objective for a summer offensive. This worked so well that when on June 19 copies of the plans for the attack on the Caucasus fell into Russian hands they

believed them authentic but were still convinced that the main attack would be on Moscow. A staff officer of the 23rd Panzer Division had been carrying the plans in a Storch and had been shot down and captured. Hitler was enraged and the XL Corps Commander General Georg Stumme and his chief of staff were immediately sacked and arrested. Stumme was later released and died of a heart attack at the Second Battle of El Alamein in North Africa.

After a long siege by the 11th Army under General Erich von Manstein the Black Sea naval base of Sevastopol fell on July 3. It had been a hard fight in which Manstein had been forced to bring in reinforcements from the 17th Army. It had cost the German and Rumanian forces 24,000 casualties but they had taken 90,000 prisoners. Hitler was impressed by the performance of the forces

ABOVE: The wrecked 305mm guns of Maxim Gorky I, the huge modern fort that covered the northern approaches to the port of Sevastopol.

under Manstein and ordered him north to undertake the siege of Leningrad. This however prevented him crossing the Kerch Strait into the Caucasus.

Following fierce street fighting, in which artillery was used at point blank range, Rostov on the Don fell on July 23. On that day Hitler issued Directive 45 for *Unternehmen Braunschweig*, the assault on the Caucasus and the oil fields of the Caspian Sea. He also instructed Army Group North to prepare for the capture of Leningrad by the beginning of September. The operation was originally code named *Feuerzauber* – Fire Magic – and then renamed *Nordlicht* – Northern Light. Despite a series of massive assaults the city held.

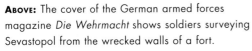

ABOVE: The cover of the German armed forces magazine *Die Wehrmacht* shows soldiers surveying Sevastopol from the wrecked walls of a fort.

ABOVE: Field Marshal von Manstein (left) confers with Colonel von Choltitz commanding the 16th Infantry Regiment near a recently captured Soviet position.

LEFT: Men of the 170th Infantry Division at the tip of the Kherson Peninsula with Soviet soldiers who were hoping to be evacuated by the Black Sea Fleet.

ABOVE: A German officer pauses by a captured barricade built to block access along a wide boulevard in central Rostov.

ABOVE: A 10.5cm howitzer opens fire by the barricade aiming at Soviet positions sited in an apartment block further down the boulevard.

BELOW: The three-man crew of a 3.7cm Pak (Sf) *auf Infanterie Schlepper* SP anti-tank gun confer with an officer during street fighting.

In Moscow Stalin was enraged at the loss of Rostov. The city of the Cossacks had initially been lost to Army Group A, then commanded by Field Marshal von Rundstedt, in a direct attack by the tanks and infantry of General von Kleist's 1st *Panzerarmee* in a direct attack in November 1941. A quick counter attack by the Soviet 9th and 37th Armies under General Timoshenko had ousted the exhausted and overstretched German forces. Von Rundstedt was ordered not to withdraw by Hitler and tendered his resignation. The action in the south had helped divert Hitler's attention from the key objective of Moscow.

For many of the Ukrainians and Don Cossacks the German forces entering the

ABOVE: Engineers manhandle a *Brückengerät* C timber and aluminium alloy pontoon unit during preliminary bridging operations across the Don at Rostov.

LEFT: An MG34 crew sited in the ruins of waterfront warehouses in Rostov covers the tranquil waters of the Don. The loss of the city enraged Stalin in 1943.

BELOW: A platoon moves into position under cover of the barricade in Rostov. No longer covered by fire, the barricade is no obstacle.

RIGHT: With his artillery scissor binoculars concealed in a corn stook Field Marshal von Bock observes the front.

BELOW: The Stuka expert General Wolfram von Richthofen, whose dive bombers blasted the way forward for the Panzers, briefs his officers.

area in the summer of 1942 were seen as liberators from the repressive government of Josef Stalin. They were greeted with the traditional offerings of bread and salt, while children offered flowers and women stood by the roads holding icons and crucifixes blessing the columns as they marched or drove by. All this was filmed and photographed by the Germans, making superb propaganda images.

On July 25 52-year-old General Friedrich Paulus, commanding the 6th Army part of Army Group B under Field Marshal Fedor von Bock, attempted to cross the Don just west of Stalingrad, but the Soviet forces blocked these attacks. Paulus was a career soldier who had served in World War I and he had been an efficient and loyal staff officer during the opening years of World War II. The 6th Army commander decided to wait until the 4th *Panzerarmee* under General Hermann Hoth was in position to drive south to assist.

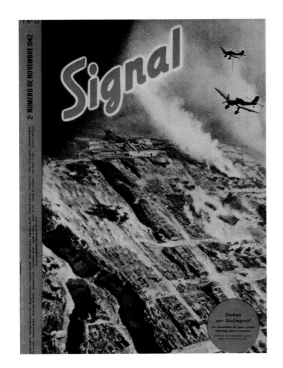

Left and below: The Stuka's eye view of Stalingrad showing the *balkas* (gullies) and the wrecked buildings and railway yards. In this terrain it was hard to identify targets accurately.

department store, Gorky theatre and Red Square. Further south was the massive concrete grain silos that would become a fortress during the fighting. Across the river a new development, Krasnaya Sloboda, was connected by ferries that delivered workers to landings stages along the shore in the southern part of the city. The NKVD or "People's Commissariat for Domestic Affairs" secret police units had been ruthless to keep them in the front line.

Political control of the 62nd Army and all

On August 10, supported by the bombers of General Freiherr Wolfram von Richthofen's *Luftlotte IV* that had been switched from supporting Army Group A, the 6th Army crossed the Don and reached the outer defences of Stalingrad.

Stalingrad had been built as a "model" town in the 1920s and 30s and included parkland and solid public buildings. The city stretched along the west bank of the Volga and consisted of two distinct districts. To the north were workers' apartments and the Dzerhezinsky Tractor, Barrikady and Krasny Oktyabr factories. The Lazur chemical plant was in the centre of a circular railway layout that was nicknamed "the tennis racket" by German aircrews. Each factory had its own schools, parks and housing development and shops.

The centre of the city was dominated by the Mamayev Kurgan – a 102-metre (334.6ft) high hill that had been a Tartar burial ground that was now a popular haunt for courting couples before the war and which divided the southern district from the north. To the south was the city centre that included the Univermag

FIELD MARSHAL FRIEDRICH PAULUS

Paulus was born in Breitenau, Melsungen District, on September 23, 1890. His family was not aristocratic and the title "von" was only given to him by Allied propaganda. A career soldier, he served in World War I and remained in the army after the war. From September 1940 to January 1942 he was a senior staff officer in the OKH. He was given command of the 6th Army in 1942 and tasked with the capture of Stalingrad. After

the 6th Army had been encircled he was promoted to Field Marshal on January 31, 1943 and surrendered with the remnants of the 6th Army in February.

On the night of June 12-13 1943 at Krasnoyarsk near Moscow the *Nationalkomitee Freies Deutschland,* (National Committee for a Free Germany), an anti-Nazi group composed of captured senior officers headed by Paulus, was set up under the control of the GRU, the Soviet Army Intelligence Service. It included German Communists like Walter Ulbricht who would play a major part in the establishment of the German Democratic Republic (DDR) (Communist East Germany) after the war. The League of German Officers (BDO) contained many veterans of the 6th Army and along with the *Nationalkomitee Freies Deutschland* worked to foment disaffection in front line troops and officers.

Paulus never saw his wife Coca again; she was imprisoned by the Nazis and released by US forces at the end of the war. Their son Alexander was killed at Anzio in 1944. Paulus was released in 1953 and died in Dresden in East Germany after a long illness in 1957. His son Ernst committed suicide aged 52.

forces within the Soviet armed forces was exercised by the *politicheskii rukovoditel, Politruk* or Commissar. One of the Commissars on the Stalingrad Front was Nikita Khruschev, the future leader of the post war Soviet Union. On the east bank of the Volga the Commissars attempted to reassure the reinforcements that were being marched to the ferries: "From this side it looks as though everything is on fire and

there's nowhere to set down your feet. But whole regiments and divisions are living there, and fighting well. They need help. They are waiting for you."

Many of the new soldiers were given a leaflet prepared by Chuikov's staff that described the tactics that would neutralise the effectiveness of the German firepower. They were urged to "Get Close to the enemy. Use craters for Cover", "Dig trenches by

ABOVE: Bombs and shells burst among the industrial buildings of Stalingrad. In the foreground are the timber-built workers' homes that would be destroyed by fire.

LEFT: SC-250 (550lb) bombs tumble away from a *Luftwaffe* bomber. Stalingrad was attacked by medium bombers like the He111 and Ju88 as well as dive bombers.

Night, Camouflage them by Day". Some survived to put these simple rules into practice and became veteran *frontoviks*, many however died standing on the western shore shivering from cold and terror as Germans bombs and shells ripped into them.

The Volga, which would prove an effective barrier to the 6th Army, was fed by a number of small tributary streams around Stalingrad. They had cut deep into the steppe soil and formed gullies or *balkas* of which the Tsaritsa and Krutoy in the southern part of the city would prove invaluable access points for Soviet soldiers who had landed from ferries.

PAVLOV'S HOUSE

Nicknamed the "Houseowner" by his comrades, Sergeant Jacob Pavlov, Hero of the Soviet Union, held a battered apartment block at Solechnaya Street for 58 days.

During the street fighting in late September Colonel Yelin, commanding the 42nd Regiment, had identified the block as a potential strongpoint. He despatched Sgt Pavlov with three men to reconnoitre and secure it. On the night of September 29 a messenger sent by Pavlov reported back to the Divisional HQ, then led 20 men to join the squad.

They prepared the building for defence, breaking down the walls between the cellars and with further reinforcements of four more men began an active defence of the building, sniping at the Germans.

By chance the group of Soviet soldiers were representative of many of the republics of the USSR and included men from Georgia, Kazakhstan, Usbekistan and the Ukraine. During the lulls in the fighting they hunted through the building and found an ancient gramophone and with it one surviving record. It was a tune unknown to them, but

as a distraction it was very welcome – so much so that they played it until the steel needle wore through the fragile disc.

The Germans continued to probe and attack the building that was now known in Soviet command posts as "Pavlov's House" – *Dom Pavlov*. It was a well chosen strong point with wide fields of fire that dominated the approaches to the Volga only 250 metres (273 yards) away.

In October four German tanks entered Lenin Square and blasted Pavlov's House. The wily sergeant moved his small force to the fourth floor or the cellar where at close range the tank guns could not reach due to the restriction on their elevation. A fighting patrol with a 14.5mm (0.57in) PTRD anti-tank rifle slipped out and knocked out one of the tanks and the survivors withdrew.

Before the fighting ended Dom Pavlov became a reference point on the 62nd Army HQ maps and Pavlov received the codename "Lighthouse". Pavlov survived the battle of Stalingrad and went on to be in the forces that captured Berlin in 1945.

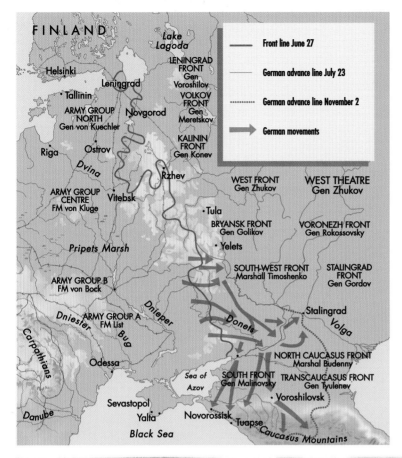

FINLAND

Lake Lagoda

Helsinki

Leningrad

Tallinin

Riga · Ostrov

Novgorod

LENINGRAD FRONT Gen Voroshilov

VOLKOV FRONT Gen Meretskov

ARMY GROUP NORTH Gen von Kuechler

Dvina

Rzhev

KALININ FRONT Gen Konev

ARMY GROUP CENTRE FM von Kluge

Vitebsk

· Tula

Pripets Marsh

ARMY GROUP B FM von Bock

WEST FRONT Gen Zhukov

WEST THEATRE Gen Zhukov

BRYANSK FRONT Gen Golikov

VORONEZH FRONT Gen Rokossovsky

· Yelets

SOUTH-WEST FRONT Marshall Timoshenko

STALINGRAD FRONT Gen Gordov

Dnieper

Dniester

ARMY GROUP A FM List

Bug

Donets

Stalingrad

Volga

Carpathians

Odessa

Sea of Azov

SOUTH FRONT Gen Malinovsky

NORTH CAUCASUS FRONT Marshal Budenny

TRANSCAUCASUS FRONT Gen Tyulenev

· Voroshilovsk

Danube

Sevastopol

Yalta ·

Novorossisk ·

Tuapse ·

Caucasus Mountains

Black Sea

Legend:
— Front line June 27
— German advance line July 23
········· German advance line November 2
➤ German movements

FAR LEFT: The collapsed roof of the tractor factory in Stalingrad, one of the modern factories close to the river Volga.

LEFT: The high water mark of German conquest. The two thrusts – one to Stalingrad and the other to the Caucasus – fatally divided the strength and resources of Army Group A and made both objectives unobtainable.

BELOW: A Krupp 1-tonne 6 x 4 model L24 43 medium truck is ferried across a Russian river on a pontoon raft.

ABOVE: Dug in on the reverse slope of a *balka* outside Stalingrad, men of the 6th Army await orders to advance.

In the hot summer months the 6th Army, part of Army Group A under List, reached Stalingrad on the Volga on August 24. To the south the summer offensive would have extended to its furthest limits by November 18. Army Group A reached the burning oil wells of Maikop on August 9 and then was into the Caucasus and within 140km (87 miles) of Grozny. The German forces were conquering territory, but were no longer rounding up huge numbers of prisoners. Photographs showed German tank crews with the snow clad Caucasus on the horizon. They reached the foothills of the mountains on August 15. Eight days later *Gebirgsjäger*, accompanied by a film crew, even climbed the 5,641-metre (18,510ft) high Mount El'brus in the Caucasus, and planted the Swastika on the highest mountain in Europe.

In 1942 the map of Europe and North Africa was coloured red as either an ally or a conquest of the Third Reich, with the only exceptions being Sweden, Spain, Portugal Switzerland, and of course Britain. It was a powerful and beguiling image, but it was soon to change. The day the Swastika flew over the Caucasus was almost the high water mark of German conquests. This would be reached on November 2, when the tanks of von Kleist's Army Group A halted eight kilometres (5 miles) west of Ordhonikidze in the Caucasus Mountains.

The pressure on the Soviet Union was so severe that secret contacts had even been made by the USSR with Germany to explore the possibility of calling a cease-fire, to be followed by peace negotiations. Stalin was on record as saying:

"In war I would deal with the Devil and his grandmother."

Paulus began to attack the outer defences of Stalingrad on August 19, but Hoth had still

LEFT: Smoke pours from burning oil tanks at the Maikop oil wells as German soldiers race through the wrecked goods yards.

ABOVE: SdKfz 250 half tracks approach Maikop. The destruction was "scorched earth" on a dramatic scale.

not joined him as his forces were held north of Tinguta.

On August 22, 1942 the XIV Panzer Corps broke through the outer defences of the Soviet 62nd Army around Stalingrad. The terrain was ideal for armoured warfare, with little cover and good visibility, but in the factories and sewers of Stalingrad this advantage would disappear. The 6th Army would lose the advantage of mobility and firepower and become bogged down in grinding street fighting. In the city territorial gains that had been measured in hundreds of kilometres would be reduced to streets, buildings and even rooms.

The 6th Army would persist since capture of Stalingrad would give the Germans control of the Volga, access to Astrakhan and the supply of petroleum from the south.

On August 24 Stalin ordered that Stalingrad should be held. The city was held by a tough and ruthless Soviet commander, General Vasili Chuikov, and overall command of the troops in the theatre was with General Zhukov. Its defence was initially a political

gesture rather than military strategy. For Stalin a city that bore his name could not be given up without a fight, while for Hitler the name of the city had a special appeal.

Chuikov took a calculated decision that the civilians in Stalingrad were not to be evacu-

ABOVE: The crew of a heavily laden half track survey the snow-covered mountains of the Caucasus. Known in local legend as "the mountains of the Moon", they were an exotic change from the rolling steppe.

ated because he asserted that Soviet soldiers would fight harder for a "living city".

Hoth finally linked up with Paulus near the airfield Pitomnik and on September 3 the German forces attempted break into the city from the west but were halted by local counter attacks.

By September 14 German attacks had forced the Soviet 62nd Army back into the industrial areas of Stalingrad that adjoined the west bank of the Volga. However, casualties had reduced the strength of the 6th Army and it was only able to attack on narrow frontages that reduced progress.

Paulus requested more reinforcements on September 20 and explained that he had been obliged to halt attacks due to increased casualties. In order to sustain attacks he had been obliged to bring in German forces on the fronts on his flanks and here Axis allies now held the line. Paulus and General von Weichs of Army Group B both warned the OKW German high command that the flanks were now increasingly vulnerable. Hitler however insisted that the attacks against Stalingrad should be continued.

By September 28 the German attackers and Soviet defenders of Stalingrad had almost reached stalemate with neither force capable of delivering a knock out.

On September 30, in a radio broadcast, Hitler spoke almost light-heartedly about a "city on the Volga", telling his audiences in the Third Reich that the city was "his".

He was almost correct. Swastiskas flew from the shattered remains of the stores and public buildings in the city and machine gunners could fire on the ferries crossing the Volga from the Soviet-held east bank.

German artillery bombarding the factories in the industrial area of the city hit the oil storage tanks on October 2. Everyone had believed that they were empty and it was therefore a shock to Soviet and German forces alike when they exploded, sending flames down the river and huge columns of black smoke into the sky.

By November 18, the men of the Soviet

BELOW: Gutted, bomb blasted and shell scarred, an industrial building in Stalingrad bears mute testimony to the ferocity of the fighting.

MARDER III *PANZERJÄGER*

Marder III *Panzerjäger* anti-tank guns used Soviet 7.62mm FK 296 anti-tank guns captured in large numbers in 1941. Ironically it was the only weapon that was capable of defeating tanks like the T34 and KV1 and KV2. The gun was mounted on a Czech 38 (t) tank chassis and thus became an effective mobile tank killer.

Armament:	76mm (2.9in); one 7.92mm MG
Armour:	20mm (max) (0.78in)
Crew:	4
Weight:	10,500kg (10.33 tons)
Hull length:	4.95m (16ft 3in)
Width:	2.15m (7ft 6in)
Height:	2.48m (8ft 1in)
Engine:	Praga EPA 6-cyl petrol 125bhp
Road speed:	42km/h (26mph)
Range:	190km (118 miles)

ABOVE: Laden with weapons and equipment, soldiers of the 6th Army slog down the dusty road to Stalingrad. Few would return after 1945.

RIGHT: Hitler boasted that he had "taken" Stalingrad and in the autumn of 1942 the 6th Army had compressed the Soviet 62nd Army under General Chuikov into a few narrow strips along the west bank of the Volga.

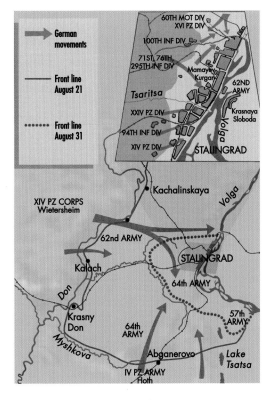

LEFT: In the southern industrial suburbs German soldiers wait for the arrival of an assault gun to support them in the next phase of their advance.

BELOW: Dug in on a dirt track in the outskirts of Stalingrad an MG34 crew covers down a road. Some of the wooden houses behind them would later become firewood.

TROUBLE AT THE TOP

In September 1942 Hitler despatched Colonel General Alfred Jodl, chief of the *Oberkommando der Wehrmachtführungsstab*, the German Armed Forces High Command, to Field Marshal Siegmund List, commander of Army Group A. He was to establish why Army Group A was making such slow progress in the capture of the Caucasus and the Caspian oil fields. The reason was simply that Army Group A lacked the resources for the mission since they were going to the 6th Army at Stalingrad. Jodl discussed the problem with List and returned on September 7 to brief Hitler. The *Führer's* reaction was to rage at Jodl, but to Hitler's surprise the normally quiet Jodl vehemently defended List. Jodl then wrote out his resignation and requested a posting to a front line command. He was persuaded by his father-in-law Field Marshal Wilhelm Keitel, the Commander-in-Chief of the OKW, *Oberkommando des Wehrmacht* (High Command of the Armed Forces), to remain in his post. Hitler was shaken by the show of opposition, refused to shake hands with Keitel and Jodl for months and stopped eating his meals with the HQ staff, preferring to dine alone.

ABOVE: Hunched in the cover of a PzKpfw III a soldier scans neighbouring buildings for Soviet positions. Tank and infantry cooperation was essential for survival in such dangerous conditions.

MOLOTOV COCKTAIL

Named in the West after the Soviet Foreign Minister Vyacheslav Molotov, this weapon is now widely known as a petrol bomb. It consisted of a thin-walled 1-litre (2.1-pint) or .75 litre (1.58-pint) bottle containing about .5 litre (1 pint) of petrol with a rag stuffed into the open neck. The petrol could be thickened with one part oil or raw rubber.

Immediately before throwing, the bottle was tipped up so that the rag was soaked with petrol and it was then lit.

When the bottle hit the target and shattered, flaming petrol would splash over an area about 2 to 3 metres square (6.5ft to 9.8ft), burning for up to five minutes. The aim was to pitch the bottle so that it landed on the rear deck of a tank and the burning petrol entered the engine space. Soviet soldiers would sometimes follow up an attack with bottles filled with petrol to stoke the fire started by the Molotov Cocktail.

Looking spectacular, its lethality varied .

LAVOCHKIN LA-5FN

Among the new Soviet Air Force fighters that made their operational debuts at Stalingrad in late 1942, the Lavochkin La-5FN proved more than a match for the Luftwaffe Bf109 fighters and by the end of the war over 10,000 had been built. It used a mixture of wood and metal in its construction that made it light and easy to maintain, and build.

Type:	Single-engined fighter
Crew:	1
Power Plant:	One 1,850hp Shvetsov Ash-82FN
Performance:	Maximum speed at 6,400m (21,000ft) 648km/h (403mph)
Range:	765km (475 miles)
Weights:	Empty 2,605kg (5,743lb) Loaded 3,360kg (7,408lb)
Dimensions:	Wing span 9.8m (32ft 2in) Length 8.67m (28ft 5in) Height 2.54m (8ft 4in)
Armament:	Two 20mm ShVAK or 23mm NS cannon in upper cowling; max bomb or rocket payload 300kg (662lb)

62nd Army only held toe holds on the west bank of the Volga but these included the huge Tractor, Barrikady and Krasny Oktyabr factories. The area was 20km (12.4 miles) deep at its deepest point and 8km (5 miles) at its narrowest.

The capture of the Mamayev Kurgan by the German 295th Infantry Division gave them a commanding view of the city. The hill was an ancient burial ground and a pre-war beauty spot and had been bitterly contested. It was only finally recaptured by the Soviet 284th Division in January 1943.

The Soviet troops had been bombed and shelled and discipline imposed by the *Narodnyy Kommissariat Vnutrennikh Del* – NKVD. The best of the German forces were now completely entangled in Stalingrad and on their northern flank on the River Don bend the front lines were held by less well equipped and trained Rumanian troops of the 3rd Rumanian Army under General Dumitrescu and the Italian 8th Army. The 4th Rumanian Army under General Constanescu held the front to the south of Stalingrad. The

ABOVE: Repairing telephone lines in an area behind the lines in which the sign warns that partisan attacks are a threat.

PETLYAKOV PE-2

The Pe-2 was a demanding aircraft to fly, but equipped several élite Soviet Guards Regiments. The most remarkable was the 125th M.M. Raskova Borisov Guards Bomber Regiment whose air and ground crew were all women. Between 1943 and 1945 the Regiment flew 1,134 sorties, with some crews flying three sorties a day, and had dropped 980,000kg of bombs. By the close of the war Soviet aircraft factories had built 11,427 Pe-2 bombers.

Type:	Dive bomber
Crew:	3 - 4
Power Plant:	Two 1,100hp Klimov M-105R
Performance:	Maximum speed at 5,000m (16,400ft) 540km/h (336mph) Range 1,500km (932 miles)
Weights:	Empty 5,876kg (12,943lb) Loaded 8,496kg (18,730lb)
Dimensions:	Wing span 17.16m (56ft 3in) Length 12.66m (41ft 6in) Height 4m (13ft 1in)
Armament:	Two fixed 7.62mm ShKAS or one 12.7mm Beresin and one 7.62mm ShKAS in the nose; one flexible 7.62mm ShKAS or one 12.7mm Beresin UBT machine gun in each dorsal and ventral position; max bomb load 1,200kg (2,645lb)

ABOVE: Laden with stores and personal kit, PzKpfw III tanks grind through a Russian village.

decision that would prove fatal was at the time probably seen as the best move in the circumstances. The Rumanian troops had fought hard at Odessa and Sevastopol in 1941 and 1942 and with the Italians could hold the flanks while better equipped, motivated an trained Germans captured Stalingrad.

With the onset of winter, due to poor administration the 6th Army did not receive the new cold weather uniforms that had been developed following the winter of 1941-42. Italian and Rumanian troops huddled in greatcoats in the snow. The uniforms were held in depots and had not been sent forward because it was thought that they had a lower priority compared to ammunition and rations necessary to prosecute the offensive.

Forty thousand fur coats, caps and boots were held in depots in Millerovo. In stores in Morosovskaia, Tormosin, Chir, Peskovatka, Tatsinskaya, Oblivskaia and Cherkovo were 2,000,000 shirts, 40,000 hats, 102,000 pairs of felt boots, 83,000 pairs of long pants, 61,000 pairs of quilted trousers, 53,000 quilted jackets, 121,000 greatcoats as well as scarves, mittens, gloves and socks.

Some exotic civilian winter clothing did reach Stalingrad and when men of the 100th Infantry Division kitted themselves out they looked as if they were off to a fancy dress

SNIPERISM

The ruthlessly efficient Soviet snipers at Stalingrad were the object of fear and hatred by German soldiers. In contrast in Moscow their operations, described as "sniperism", were celebrated by the Soviet propaganda machine. Many were experienced hunters and were equipped with a Mosin Model 1891/30 rifle with a x 4 PE telescopic sight. The M1891/30 weighed 4kg (8.8lb) empty, had a muzzle velocity of 811m/s (2,661f/s) and though a modernisation of an old design it was robust and reliable. The sights were offset mounted on the left of the receiver to allow the empty cases to be ejected when the bolt was worked. Until 1930 the iron sights on the rifle were graduated in the archaic linear measurement of arshins (0.71m) but the Soviet government redesigned the back sight in metres and so the modified weapon became the 1891/30. The other rifle issued to snipers was the Tokarev SVT1940 automatic rifle fitted with a x 3.5 PV telescopic sight. It weighed 3.95kg (8.7lb) and had a 20-round box magazine. Early models were unreliable, but the 1940 version was modified and eventually two million were manufactured. Soviet snipers usually worked in pairs at a low tactical level assigned directly to companies and platoons. Though popularised after the war the sniper duel between Vasily Zaitsev, who had killed 149 Germans, and Major Koenig, the head of the German sniper school at Zossen, that was the basis for the $85 million film "Enemy at the Gates" released in 2001, was probably a Soviet propaganda invention. Zaitsev, played by Jude Law, existed but the sinister Koenig, played by Ed Harris, was fictional.

A WAR BALLAD

The Soviet war correspondent Alexei Surkov composed a song during the siege that in official circles was condemned as "too negative" but to *frontoviks* it summed up their feelings.

> "In our bunker the log fire burns
> Weeping resin, it sputters and sighs
> The accordion's haunting refrain
> Sings of you, your smile and your eyes,
> We are light years apart
> And divided by snow-covered steppes
> Though the road to your side is so hard
> To death's door it's four easy steps".

LEFT: A Soviet 50mm light mortar crew fires from within ruins in Stalingrad that screen its position from observation and fire.

LIEUTENANT GENERAL VASILY IVANOVICH CHUIKOV

Born at Serebryannye Prudy near Moscow on February 12,1900, Vasily Chuikov was the son of peasants, and worked as a mechanic apprentice from the age of 12. At the age of 18, after the Russian Revolution, he joined the Red Army. By a strange historic twist his first experience of combat in the Civil War was in 1918 at Tsaritsyn, the city that became Stalingrad and is now Volgagrad, and by the following year he was a member of the Communist Party and a regimental commander. He served against Kolchak in the Russo-Polish war of 1920.

Chuikov graduated from the M.V. Frunze Military Academy in 1925, took part in the Soviet invasion of Poland (1939) and in the Russo-Finnish War (1939-40), and had just finished serving as military attaché in China

when he was called to Stalingrad to be in command of the 62nd Army in the city's defence.

At Stalingrad Chuikov allegedly declared: "We shall hold the city or die here." He subsequently led his forces, redesignated the 8th Guards Army, into the Donets Basin and then into the Crimea and north to Belarussia before spearheading the Soviet drive to Berlin. Chuikov personally accepted the German surrender of Berlin on May 1, 1945.

After the war he served with the Soviet occupation forces in Germany (1945-53).

T-34/85

The turret of this improved version of the successful Soviet T-34 design could accommodate three men, so now the commander could concentrate on his proper role rather than attempting to fire the main armament as had been the case with the T-34/76. Armed with a powerful 85mm ZIS S-53 gun, the T34/85 was described at the time by the Germans as "the best tank in the world". It would prove a formidable opponent in the Korean War and soldier on into the 1970s in South East Asia.

Armament:	85mm (3.3in), 2 x 7.62mm DT MG
Armour:	18-60mm (0.71-2.36in)
Crew:	5
Weight:	31,500kg (31 tons)
Hull length:	8.07m (26ft 5in)
Width:	3.21m (10ft 6in)
Height:	2.56m (8ft 5in)
Engine:	500hp V-2-34 12-cylinder water-cooled diesel 500hp
Road speed:	50km/h (31mph)
Range:	300km (186.3 miles)

SU-76

With its open top and rear the SU76M was not popular with its four-man crews, however, with the exception of the T-34 it was the most widely produced armoured vehicle in the USSR during World War II. It was fast, mobile and so an effective tank hunter. The Soviet crews nicknamed it "Sucha" or the "Bitch" because of its spartan interior and as a pun on its designation.

Armament:	One ZIS-3 76mm (2.9in) gun
Armour:	25mm (1in)
Crew:	4
Weight:	10,600kg (10.4 tons)
Hull length:	4.88m (16ft)
Width:	2.73m (8ft 11in)
Height:	2.17m (7ft 1in)
Engine:	Two GAZ six cylinder petrol engines each developing 70hp
Road speed:	45km/h (28mph)
Range:	450km (280miles)

ISU-152

The formidable ISU-152 that used the chassis of the KV1 heavy tank entered service just in time for the fighting at Kursk. The big Soviet assault gun took the powerful 152mm (5.9in) M1937 gun howitzer, with its distinctive multi baffle muzzle brake, as its main armament. The howitzer fired a 48.8kg (107.6lb) Armour Piercing High Explosive shell that could penetrate 124mm (4.8in) of armour at 1,000 metres, with an HE round it could reach out to 17,265 metres (10.7 miles).

Armament:	One152mm (5.9in) howitzer; 12.7mm anti-aircraft MG
Armour:	35mm to 100mm (1.38in to 3.94in)
Crew:	5
Weight:	45,500kg (44.7 tons)
Hull length:	9.80m (32ft 1in)
Width:	3.56m (11ft 8in)
Height:	2.52m (8ft 3in)
Engine:	One V-12 diesel engine developing 520bhp
Road speed:	37km/h (23mph)
Range:	180km (112 miles)

party and not the front line. The Army reporter Heinz Schröter noted grimly: "The scenes which took place at this depot were amongst the few events at which the Stalingrad soldiers were able to laugh."

As far back as September 1942 Stalin and STAVKA – the Soviet High Command – had realised that the 6th Army was out on a limb. However, the first priority would be an attempt to relieve the besieged northern city of Leningrad. These attacks were launched in August and ended by September. The plan for Stalingrad would be a double envelopment by attacks on the vulnerable flanks to the north and south.

On November 11 the Germans in Stalingrad had one final effort at eliminating the 62nd Army in savage fighting in the city.

Chuikov was urged to hang on.

His men were going into action inspired or terrified by three slogans:

"Every man a fortress!"

"There's no ground left behind the Volga!"

"Fight or die!"

ABOVE: In late summer German mechanised and mounted troops move eastwards. In a few months the horses would be slaughtered and eaten.

DER TOTALER KRIEG

Our troops in the approaches of Stalingrad have gone on the offensive against German forces. The offensive was undertaken at two sectors in the northwest and south of Stalingrad...our troops have advanced 35 to 40 miles in three days of intense fighting in which they overcame enemy resistance.

STAVKA Special Announcement

Monday November 23, 1942

On November 19 1942 Zhukov launched Operation Uranus. He had positioned the South West Front under General Nikolai Vatutin consisting of the 63rd Army, 1st Guards Army and 21st Army, a total of one million men, 13,500 guns and 894 tanks, opposite the Rumanian and Italian armies. After a short but intense

ABOVE: Holding his P08 Luger, a German NCO surveys the wreckage of a Soviet position in the dust and chaos of Stalingrad.

ABOVE: Grim-faced and laden with weapons and ammunition, a German soldier makes his way through one of the ruined factories.

ABOVE: A German officer surrounded by his platoon scans the buildings for snipers.

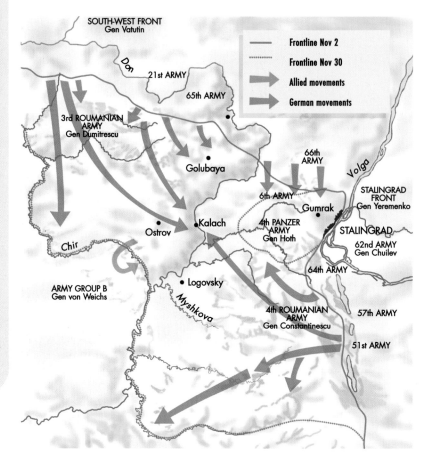

SOUTH-WEST FRONT
Gen Vatutin

Frontline Nov 2
Frontline Nov 30
Allied movements
German movements

Don

21st ARMY

65th ARMY

3rd ROUMANIAN
ARMY
Gen Dumitrescu

Golubaya

66th
ARMY

Volga

6th ARMY

Gumrak

STALINGRAD
FRONT
Gen Yeremenko

Kalach

4th PANZER
ARMY
Gen Hoth

STALINGRAD

Ostrov

62nd ARMY
Gen Chuilev

Chir

64th ARMY

Logovsky

ARMY GROUP B
Gen von Weichs

Myshkova

4th ROUMANIAN
ARMY
Gen Constantinescu

57th ARMY

51st ARMY

LEFT: Operation Uranus cuts off the 6th Army at Stalingrad. Hitler's obsession not to yield captured territory would doom the 6th Army to a slow freezing death.

BELOW LEFT: Towing their MG34 on a simple cargo sledge are German soldiers in winter uniforms. This kit was not supplied to the 6th Army.

BELOW: Mail call – a critical morale boost for soldiers who were now thousands of miles from home.

ABOVE: Soviet anti-aircraft guns ringed the 6th Army, engaging transport aircraft as they made the hazardous flight into the pocket in Staingrad.

bombardment the Soviets' tanks and infantry tore through the Axis forces. The 21st Army initially had a hard fight with the Rumanian Army on the northern Don, but punched through and swung south behind the German 6th Army.

On November 20 the Stalingrad Front attacked and by the end of the day had penetrated up to 50km (31 miles). Aware now that it was under a serious threat, the 6th Army headquarters was moved to Nizhne-Chirskave on the River Chir. A day later Paulus ordered the HQ to move eastward to the airfield at Gumrak, closer to Stalingrad.

In five days the 26th Tank Corps of the 21st Army had linked up with men of the 4th Tank Corps of the Stalingrad Front south of Stalingrad, at Kalatch on the Don, in November and this closed the trap on the 6th Army. Though the next priority was to destroy the 4th Panzerarmee and 6th Army inside the Stalingrad pocket, the Soviet forces were still on the move and relatively under strength. The reduction would take time.

On November 26 Hitler issued orders that the 6th Army make no attempt to break out from Stalingrad. *Reichsmarschall* Hermann Göring, head of the *Luftwaffe*, assured the

RIGHT: *Reichsmarschall* Hermann Göring who promised Hitler that the *Luftwaffe* could keep the 6th Army supplied by air as had been done with smaller pockets in Russia in 1941-42.

Führer that it could supply the trapped army – a promise beyond the capability of the *Luftwaffe*. The 6th Army staff estimated that the pocket would need to receive 762,000kg (750 tons) of supplies a day to survive. Not only did the *Luftwaffe* not have sufficient aircraft, but only one of the seven airstrips around Stalingrad could operate at night – critical in the long Russian winter nights.

The lumbering Ju52 transports did manage

GENERAL NIKOLAI F. VATUTIN

Born in 1901, Vatutin was Head of General Staff Operations when Germany invaded the USSR. He served with distinction at the Battle of Moscow in 1941. He was appointed commander of the South West Front in 1942. His front encircled the 6th Army at Stalingrad. Following the surrender of the German army his forces pushed deep into the occupied interior of the Ukraine. In July 1943 he commanded the Voronezh Front at Kursk. His subsequent offensive liberated Kharkov on August 22 and much of the Ukraine. On November 6 his command, renamed the 1st Ukrainian Front, captured Kiev and kept the pressure on the Germans throughout the winter. On February 29 1944 Vatutin was ambushed by anti-Soviet Ukrainian Nationalist partisans near Rovno and fatally wounded. (Zhukov called these partisans "Bandera bandits", after Stepan Bandera, the Ukrainian nationalist leader who sided with the Germans.)

ABOVE: Messerschmitt Bf109 fighters run up their engines. Soviet fighters were better suited to the harsh conditions of the East.

to fly out some casualties and bring in supplies, but intense anti-aircraft fire and long flights made it an increasingly hazardous journey. The best delivery that was achieved by the *Luftwaffe* was on December 19 when it flew in 254,000kg (250 tons). The average during the siege when airfields were open was 91,440kg (90 tons) a day.

On November 27 Field Marshal von Manstein was appointed to command the newly formed Army Group Don. The force was composed of one *Luftwaffe*, four Panzer and six infantry divisions along with the remnants of a number of Rumanian formations. Von Manstein was ordered to break into the encirclement to relieve the 6th Army.

WAFFEN-SS

The *Waffen-SS* – Armed SS – was the military arm and largest branch of the SS. The force would eventually number 39 divisions and through its ranks would pass nearly one million men of 15 nationalities.

The *Waffen-SS* was formed in 1940 with the SS Divisions *Leibstandarte-SS Adolf Hitler, Das Reich* and *Totenkopf*. By the close of the war the SS had become a huge organisation that ran the concentration and extermination camps, race and ethnicity and Reich and overseas intelligence and security. At the Nuremberg trials all members of the SS, with the exception of the *Waffen-SS*, were declared to be war criminals.

The *Waffen-SS* would take part in 12 major battles and was noted for its tough fighting qualities and aggressive leadership. The premier formation of the *Waffen-SS*, the *Leibstandarte Adolf Hitler* – Adolf Hitler's Bodyguard – provided guards of honour for visiting VIPs before the war. The *Waffen-SS* saw little action in Poland but fought in France, the Balkans and Russia. The *Waffen-SS* troops assert that they were élite soldiers but their record in the fighting on the Eastern Front and in Western Europe shows that though their courage and skill is not disputed, they were also guilty of excesses against civilians and prisoners.

At the beginning there were strict racial and physical standards for soldiers in the *Waffen-SS*, however, search for manpower obliged Himmler's recruiters to look for ethnic Germans in Europe and later even Yugoslavs, Italians and Ukrainians. Most of the foreign formations were of little value in the field.

The *Waffen-SS* practice of tattooing a soldier's blood group under his left armpit, while making excellent sense for combat first aid, also meant that members of the *Waffen-SS* could not disguise themselves as soldiers in the *Wehrmacht* if they were captured. On the Eastern Front few soldiers of the *Waffen-SS* survived capture.

ABOVE: In winter camouflage uniforms, with coloured identification bands on the sleeves, a German patrol outside the pocket moves through the snow.

Instead of attacking along the line of the Don at its junction with the Chir, the most direct route to Stalingrad, in an operation code named "Winter Storm" he chose as his axis the Kotelnikovo-Stalingrad railway to the south. He did not wait for all the units to concentrate but, in order to ensure surprise, intended to attack on December 3. However on November 30 there were renewed Soviet attacks to clear the German forces from the lower Chir. Manstein was forced to detach formations intended for "Winter Storm" but halted the Soviet attacks.

RIGHT: A German officer passes instruction over a field telephone. Even though telephone lines were often cut by shellfire, they were secure.

ABOVE: PzKpfw IV tanks halt in the cover of a Russian village during Operation Winter Storm, the attempt by Field Marshal von Manstein to relieve Stalingrad.

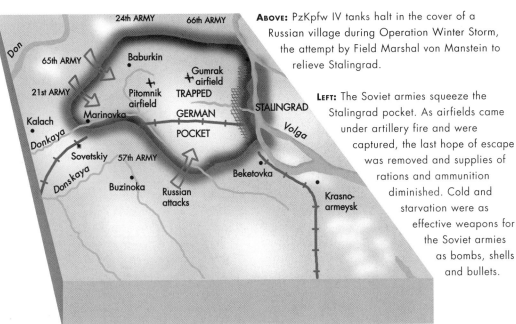

LEFT: The Soviet armies squeeze the Stalingrad pocket. As airfields came under artillery fire and were captured, the last hope of escape was removed and supplies of rations and ammunition diminished. Cold and starvation were as effective weapons for the Soviet armies as bombs, shells and bullets.

RIGHT: Hundreds of miles to the north Spanish troops on the Eastern Front were secure in reinforced concrete bunkers near Leningrad.

At Stalingrad the Don and Stalingrad Fronts launched heavy attacks on December 3 to break into the pocket. Their objective was to link up at the airfield at Gumrak. After five days heavy fighting they had made virtually no headway and the attacks were called off.

A new operation code named "Ring" was proposed. It would be a two-phase operation. Phase one would be to liquidate the south and west parts of the pocket and the final phase would be a general assault against the remainder of the pocket. Ring was planned to begin on December 16.

The Germans launched "Winter Storm" on December 12. Troops of Group Hoth commanded by General Hermann Hoth including soldiers of the elite *Waffen-SS* initially made good progress. They then encountered fierce resistance from the 5th Shock Army which bought time that allowed troops to be deployed from the Stalingrad pocket to take up blocking positions.

On December 16 the Soviet Voronezh and South West Fronts launched "Little Saturn", an attack on the Italian 8th Army on the Chir. The Italians were quickly overwhelmed and the key re-supply airfield at Tatsinskaya was captured.Three days later, to the south, Hoth's troops pushed to within 30km (18.6 miles) of the Stalingrad pocket. Manstein urged Paulus to break out to the south, but the commander of the 6th Army was only prepared to release some tanks without infantry support. Group Hoth attempted to breakthrough until December 23, but a day later the Soviet counter-offensive broadened. The Soviet 51st Army punched through the Rumanians, while the 5th Tank Army crossed the Chir. Manstein's thrust was in danger of being enveloped.

ABOVE RIGHT: The crews of StuG IIIs warm up around an oil drum brazier and slice tinned meat to cook a rudimentary meal during a break in "Winter Storm". The soldiers nicknamed the meat "Old Man" from the initials "AM" on the tin.

RIGHT: Accompanied by a PzKpfw III, an infantry patrol makes its way across snow-covered fields. The men are widely spaced as a precaution against artillery fire.

LEFT: A heroic artist's impression in *Signal* of the final fighting in the northern pocket in Stalingrad.

RIGHT: A nurse prepares a meal for wounded soldiers convalescing in Germany in this propaganda photograph of Christmas at home.

BELOW: One of the superb cartoons produced by the Krokodil team in Moscow that both demonised and ridiculed the Nazis.

On Christmas Day the Propaganda Ministry broadcast greetings from the crew of a U-boat in the Atlantic, men of the *Afrika Korps* in North Africa, the garrison of the Atlantic Wall and, over a crackling radio link, the men of Stalingrad, "the front on the Volga". Their voices then blended together in *Stille Nacht*, the classic German Christmas carol. It was dramatic and very moving – and faked up in radio studios in Berlin.

The Soviet Army propaganda teams were also making use of the radio. With the recorded sound of a metronome clicking out sixty seconds a voice would announce:

"Every minute a German soldier dies in Stalingrad."

On December 28 Hitler sanctioned a withdrawal by Army Groups Don and A to the line Konstantinovsk-Salsk-Armavir. This effectively doomed Stalingrad because the German front line was now 300km (186.4 miles) to the

west. If the 6th Army had been allowed to attempt a break out during "Winter Storm" they might have saved many lives.

Rokossovsky offered Paulus surrender terms on January 8 but they were rejected. Two days later the Soviet offensive rolled into action squeezing the pocket from west to east. The 65th Army advanced 10km (6.2 miles) on the first day against determined German resistance and counter-attacks. To the north and south only limited penetrations were achieved.

On the morning of the attack Colonel Herbert Selle, who commanded the pioneers, military engineers, in the 6th Army, encountered Paulus at his HQ.

The general noticed Selle and said:
"What do you say to all this?"
"I agree with what all the other older staff officers say, Sir."
"And what is that?"
"The Herr General should have disobeyed orders, but the opportunity was let slip. As early as November the Herr General should have wirelessed: 'I fight this battle with and for the Sixth Army. Until it is over, my head belongs to them. After the battle, my *Führer*, it belongs to you.'"

Paulus looked at Selle:
"I am aware that military history has already passed judgement on me."

On January 12 the western salient of the

ABOVE: The raw cold shows on the faces of a German patrol. The man on the left has the big holster for a signal pistol.

pocket had been overrun. It had cost the Don Front 26,000 casualties and over 125 tanks. A day later Karpovka airfield in the south of the pocket was captured. There were now only six airfields available for supply or evacuation.

Hitler ordered the highly capable Field Marshal Erhard Milch to take over the air resupply operations to Stalingrad on January 14. The daily delivery rate had dropped to 4,064kg (40 tons) a day as aircraft struggled over longer distances against increased Soviet opposition. On the day that Milch moved to Manstein's HQ at Taganrog on January 16 the airfield of Pitomnik in the

LEFT: A Waffen-SS SdKfz 251 with the crew clad in superior Waffen SS-issue fur-lined parkas. Helmets are slung on the hull.

middle of the pocket fell to the Soviet 21st Army. Incredibly Milch had managed to increase deliveries to 60,960kg (60 tons) per day and a new airfield was hastily constructed within the pocket.

Milch was a capable officer who had served in the air force in World War I. He collaborated with Göring, who chose to ignore the fact that Milch's mother was Jewish, in the establishment of the *Luftwaffe* in the 1930s. From 1941–44 he was the *Luftzeugmeister* (Air Inspector General).

The pace of the operations was beginning to tell on the Soviet forces and their rudimentary logistic back up and Rokossovsky wanted to call a halt for two to three days. Stalin urged that they continue as the exhausted and starving German soldiers were offering less resistance with each day.

The airfield at Gumrak fell on January 22 and Paulus signalled that rations and ammunition were now dangerously low and made an oblique plea to be allowed to order his forces to surrender. In the ruins of the city the Soviet 21st Army linked up with the men of the 62nd Army – the German 6th Army was now split into two pockets in the north and south of Stalingrad.

The last German aircraft to make the flight to Stalingrad, a Heinkel He111 carrying 19 wounded men and seven bags of mail, flew out of the pocket on January 23. Some supplies were air dropped in the last week. It is reported that the last letters from Stalingrad were never delivered but impounded on the orders of Goebbels. They were analysed to assess the morale of the troops within the pocket. Some expressed belief in the ultimate victory of the Third Reich and the *Führer*, Adolf Hitler, others were bleak protests of anger and disillusionment. The "Stalingrad mood" was divided into five groups:

a) In favour of the way the war was being
   conducted 21%
b) Dubious 4.4%
c) Sceptical, deprecatory 57.1%
d) Actively against 3.4%
e) No opinion, indifferent 33.0%

In the southern pocket Paulus moved his HQ to the basement of the Univermag department store. It was from here that the Swastika had flown in the early autumn. By now food was in such short supply that orders were issued that the 30,000 wounded in the pocket were not to receive rations. Many men had already died of starvation and the bitter cold.

In a final superb gesture on January 29-30 some 124 *Luftwaffe* bombers and transport aircraft delivered rations and ammunition in a night drop.

On January 30 there was a final signal from the 6th Army HQ to Hitler's HQ:

"A thousand years hence Germans will speak of this battle with reverence and awe. The

ABOVE: A scout from the 62nd Army jumps from a gutted building during the final stages of the fighting in Stalingrad.

ABOVE RIGHT: 6th Army staff officers including General Dr Korfes and General von Seydlitz Kurzbach immediately after their surrender.

RIGHT: Like a scene from the 100 Years War German soldiers make their way into captivity past the ruins of Stalingrad.

Swatiska flag is still flying above Stalingrad. May our battle be an example to the present and future generations, that they must never capitulate even in a hopeless situation, for them Germany will emerge victorious."

On January 31 at 19.45 local time Paulus surrendered after his HQ in the basement of

ABOVE: Prisoners trudge past the huge Stalingrad grain silo that had been both a landmark and a fortress during the fighting in 1942.

the Univermag building had been surrounded. Gaunt and exhausted, the recently promoted Field Marshal emerged with his staff to surrender to the men of General Chuikov's 62nd Army. Hitler had stated that no German Field Marshal had ever surrendered and hoped that Paulus would commit suicide rather than surrender. Some officers and his staff did.

General von Hartman, commander of the 71st Division, walked out to a railway embankment in full view of the Soviet lines and began firing a carbine in their direction. A few minutes later his wish was granted as he was hit in the head by a sniper's bullet.

LEFT: The Red flag over Red Square. A victorious Soviet soldier waves the flag from the 6th Army HQ at the Univermag store.

Many of the starving wounded used pistols and grenades to end their lives rather than face a brutal death at the hands of Soviet soldiers.

Back in Germany at a luncheon conference Hitler snapped: "The duty of the men at Stalingrad is to be dead."

On February 2 the XI Corps under General Strecker in the northern pocket surrendered. It had been reduced to a small area around the Tractor Factory and was subject to a final bombardment by Soviet artillery batteries so dense that each gun was only three metres (nine feet) apart. The Russians were enraged by this resistance and many Germans who attempted to surrender were shot or clubbed to death. Just before the XI Corps HQ was overrun General Strecker signalled to Hitler:

"11th Corps and its divisions have fought to the last man against vastly superior forces.

ABOVE: Field Marshal Paulus arrives at General Chuikov's HQ for his preliminary interrogation following the surrender. Paulus survived captivity, unlike many of the men of the 6th Army.

Long Live Germany"

Figures for the Russian victory at Stalingrad are hard to establish but German and Axis losses were in the region of 1.5 million men, 3,500 tanks, 12,000 guns and mortars, 75,000 vehicles and 3,000 aircraft. Of the prisoners only 5,000 survivors returned to Germany in the 1950s. Many had died in grim camps from starvation, disease and overwork.

At Moscow in the winter of 1941-42 Nazi Germany was fated not to win World War II; at Stalingrad a year later it was doomed to lose it. 1942 was a significant year not only for the victory at Stalingrad, it was the year that Soviet war production overtook that of

LEFT: Heaps of German corpses gathered for mass burial after the surrender. Cold and starvation had killed as effectively as Soviet guns.

RIGHT: In the safety of the main German lines the crew of a 7.5cm StuG III snatch a quick meal.

BELOW RIGHT: German prisoners march eastwards. The Stalingrad defeat was a profound psychological shock to Nazi Germany, that since 1939 had enjoyed almost continuous victories.

Germany – 24,000 to 4,800 in armoured vehicles and 21,700 to 14,700 in aircraft.

In Germany the nation was in shock from the huge losses. Goebbels mobilised the press and radio to unite the nation in martial grief.

Four days of mourning were ordered. Detailed instructions to the press told them that the enemy were to be called "Bolsheviks" not "Russians".

"The whole of German propaganda must

DER TOTALER KRIEG – TOTAL WAR

The term Total War was first used by the World War I general and post-war nationalist politician Erich von Ludendorff in his book published in 1935 entitled *Der Totaler Krieg* (translated into English as "The Nation at War"). His thesis was that Total War was a type of warfare that demanded "the strength of the people".

The mobilisation in the name of Total War that followed the defeat at Stalingrad included the drafting of women into the munitions industry and armed forces. Cultural life came to a virtual standstill, with the exception of light entertainment that would help to boost the industrial and munition workers' morale.

create a myth out of the heroism of Stalingrad," he explained, it was: "to become one of the most treasured possessions in German history."

On February 18, 1943 he made a speech at the *Sportpalastrede* (Sport Palace) in Berlin

that set the new tone for the war. Under a huge banner that read *Totaler Krieg für Zester Krieg* – Total War for Shortest War – he carried his picked audience with him in a powerful speech in which they pledged themselves for combat and sacrifice.

Sweating and hoarse, Goebbels hurled ten questions at the fanaticised crowd, each one demanding new sacrifices. Like a Greek chorus the audience responded to his demands.

"Do you want total war?"

"Yes," came the roared response.

"Are you determined to follow the *Führer* and fight for victory whatever the cost?"

"Ja!" – Yes! – they bellowed back.

The last question he posed was:

"Do you want total war?"

When the affirmation was roared back Goebbels summed up with the words of the great call to war from the Prussian war against Napoleon in 1812.

"Let our war-cry be:

'Now the People Rise Up and Storm Break Loose!'"

ABOVE: Dr Goebbels, the Third Reich Propaganda Minister and master of "spin", whose speeches and writings helped sustain German domestic morale throughout the war.

KHARKOV ARMOURED ANVIL

The troops of General Golikov have captured Kharkov. On Tuesday Soviet artillery, brought from Zhopozhnikov and moved into position around Kharkov, aimed three hours of devastating fire at the German positions... Two German Panzer divisions took extremely heavy losses as Russian assault artillery followed hard in the wake of Russian tanks.

Soviet Information Bureau Wednesday February 17, 1943, Moscow.

On January 3, 1943 the Germans began an urgent retreat from the Caucasus. Stalin had ordered his generals to drive for Rostov to trap the German forces of Army Groups A and Don that had driven south east to capture the oil fields in 1942. Operation Leap proposed by Lt General Nikolai Vatutin commanding the South West Front would have locked the Germans into the Donets Basin.

In fierce fighting on the Don River on January 14 the men of the 2nd Hungarian Army suffered 70 per cent casualties. Despite these losses Hitler demanded that Hungary should provide more troops for the Eastern Front.

RIGHT: General Nikolai F. Vatutin who commanded the Voronezh Front at Kursk but died at the end of the war when his vehicle was ambushed by Ukrainian nationalist partisans.

On January 25 Stalin issued an Order of the Day to his troops congratulating them and giving them the inspirational slogan: "Onward to defeat the German occupationists". He had promoted Zhukov to the rank of Marshal a week earlier – Stalin too, with no military training, decided that he would become a Marshal.

On February 16, 1943 the Ukrainian city of Kharkov fell to General Filip Golikov's Voronezh Front and General Nikolayev Vatutin's South West Front as the Soviet offensive that had surrounded Stalingrad continued to roll westwards.

Hitler had demanded that Kharkov, the third most important city in the USSR, should be held by three *Waffen-SS Panzer* Divisions, but *GenObst der Waffen-SS* Paul "Papa" Hausser ignored the order and pulled his troops out to the south. After driving 186km (115.6 miles) they linked up with General Hermann Hoth's 4th *Panzerarmee*. The *Waffen-SS* divisions then reversed their course and were back in the city on March 9 intent on restoring their honour. Hoth had ordered them to by-pass the city but they plunged into Kharkov on March 11 and in three days of savage fighting had recaptured it.

The operation at Kharkov was part of a

LEFT: Hungarian troops in the bitter winter of 1942-43. As casualties mounted Hitler made constant demands that Axis allies like Hungary should provide more troops for the East.

RIGHT: At a safe distance from the gun pit, members of a Hungarian 2cm Flak deployed in the ground support role, cook a goulash in the spring of 1943.

counter-attack against the southern flank of the two Soviet Fronts by Army Group South commanded by Field Marshal Manstein that inflicted heavy losses and forcing them back behind the river Donets. To the south Operation Leap had over-extended itself and ended when on February 18 the 1st *Panzer Armee* demolished Vatutin's mobile group.

Part of the reason for Manstein's triumph may have been his close tactical control of the fast-moving battle. There were no long encoded Enigma signals back to Hitler's HQ at Rastenburg in East Prussia. It was signals like these that were the undoing of German plans since they were intercepted and decoded as part of the ULTRA operation at Bletchley Park.

On March 1 Army Group Centre began an operation code named Buffalo – the phased withdrawal from the Rzhev salient opposite Moscow. Even Hitler agreed that it was no longer a credible threat to the Soviet capital. By March 23 the Germans halted on a line from Velizh to Kirov. They had cut their frontage by nearly 400km and freed enough troops to keep Rokossovsky in check.

Despite the huge losses following the surrender at Stalingrad, Hitler remained optimistic. He had 3.07 million soldiers in Russia, slightly more than in June 1941, and new weapons and equipment were reaching them in the front line. Operation Buffalo had

ABOVE RIGHT: Two Waffen-SS PzKpfw IVs and a Marder III fire down a boulevard in Kharkov during the fight for the city.

RIGHT: PzKpfw IVs move past piles of cleared snow. Kharkov was hailed as a victory that compensated for the loss of Stalingrad.

FAR RIGHT: A column of up-armoured *Waffen-SS* SdKfz 251 half tracks roll through Kharkov following the capture of the city in 1943.

RIGHT: "One Fight – One Victory." A propaganda poster commemorates the anniversary of the seizing of power in an attempt to boost morale.

SS-OBERGRUPPENFÜHRER UND GENERAL DER WAFFEN-SS PAUL HAUSSER

Born in Brandenburg on October 7 1880, Paul Hausser served with distinction in World War I, winning the Iron Cross 1st and 2nd Class. After the war he served with the *Reichswehr*, reaching the rank of Lt General, before retiring in 1932. He joined the SS-VT and became inspector of the *SS-Junkerschule*. In 1939 he was an observer with a joint Army/SS Panzer Division, *"Kempf"*, in Poland. The SS-VT was formed into a division with Hausser in command and he led it through battles in the West and Operation *Barbarossa*. During his command of SS Division *Reich* in Russia Hausser was awarded the Knight's Cross on August 8 1941. Severely wounded, he lost an eye in the East. After recovering, he commanded the II SS Panzer Corps in the fighting at Kharkov in 1943. He led this formation at Kursk in the summer of 1943 and received Oakleaves to his Knight's Cross July 28 1943. The Corps, now composed of the 9th and 10th SS Panzer Divisions, was then stationed in the West and fought at Normandy in 1944. Hausser remained with the Corps when it was encircled at Falaise to ensure that as many men as possible escaped from the pocket. Swords were added to his Knight's Cross on August 26 1944. He ended the war on the staff of Field Marshal Albert Kesselring. Hausser died on December 21 1972 at Ludwigsburg.

ABOVE RIGHT: A StuG III with equipment loaded on the rear deck passes a shallow MG42 post dug into the frozen ground.

RIGHT: German soldiers examine a downed Yakovlev Yak-9. It was armed with one 20mm ShVAK cannon firing through the propeller hub and one 12.7mm Berezin UB machine gun.

yielded an extra army, the 9th Army, which under the vigorous command of the monocled General Walther Model had for 14 months held the toughest part of the Eastern Front, the line around Rzhev.

Fighting in Russia normally slowed down with the spring thaw that produced immobility as the roads turned to soft mud. After the victory at Kharkov the front line stabilised into a huge Soviet salient 190km (118 miles) wide and 120km (74.5 miles) deep that had

OCCUPIED UKRAINE

The German-occupied Ukraine was split into three sectors, of which the bulk came under the administration of Gauleiter Erich Koch, the *Reichskommissariat* Ukraine. Koch, a fanatical Nazi and a crude and brutal man, described himself as a "brutal dog". His task was, he said: "to suck from Ukraine all the goods we can get hold of, without consideration for the feelings or the property of the Ukrainians." Koch declared: "If I find a Ukrainian who is worthy of sitting at the same table with me, I must have him shot." He closed schools on the ground that Ukrainians did not need education and deported many thousands in Europe as slave labourers.

Koch, with his toothbrush moustache and brown uniform with red armband, was the most extreme example of the *Goldfasan* – the Golden Pheasant – as front line soldiers nicknamed the party administrators in the East. His brutality was so extreme that it even provoked opposition from the *Waffen-SS*.

The Ukraine suffered particularly harshly in World War II. For every village like Oradour in France or Lidice in Czechoslovakia that was destroyed, some 250 villages with their inhabitants suffered a similar fate in the Ukraine. Over 16,000 industrial plants and 28,000 collective farms were destroyed and direct material damage constituted over 40% of the USSR's wartime losses.

By the end of the war starvation, executions and death in combat had killed over seven million Ukrainians.

the railway city of Kursk at its centre.

The salient was an open plain broken by *balkas*, copses, villages, streams and rivers. Standing crops made visibility difficult and the ground rose to the north, which favoured the defenders. As elsewhere in the USSR, the roads were unmetalled and could deteriorate in bad weather and heavy usage.

The planned German summer offensive of 1943 aimed to pinch out the Kursk bulge with attacks from the north by Army Group Centre under Field Marshal Günther Hans von Kluge

ABOVE RIGHT: PzKpfw IV Ausf G tanks move across a winter landscape. In the absence of deep snow these tanks are not fitted with the wider track to reduce ground pressure and give better traction.

RIGHT: German soldiers examine the grim remains of a T-34/76D knocked out in the fighting in the spring of 1943. The tank had a new hexagonal turret, that eliminated the vulnerable rear overhang, and two turret hatches on previous models.

KHARKOF ARMOURED ANVIL

FIELD MARSHAL GÜNTHER HANS VON KLUGE "CLEVER HANS"

Born in Posen on October 30 1882 Kluge joined the army and served in World War I. He was in retirement in 1939, but following his recall he commanded Army Group VI in Poland and following the successful campaign in France in 1940 was promoted to Field Marshal. He commanded Army Group Centre in Russia in 1942 where the soldiers under his command, punning on his name, nicknamed him "Clever Hans". Von Kluge was not an anti-Nazi, but was never enthusiastic about Hitler. Von Kluge was injured in a vehicle accident in 1943 in Russia and after a disastrous performance in France in 1944 he committed suicide on August 18 1944 on the site of the Franco-Prussian battlefield of Metz.

and the south by Army Group South under Field Marshal Erich von Manstein. The attacks would be code-named *Unternehmen Zitadelle* – Operation Citadel. The attack would encircle and destroy the Soviet Central and Voronezh Fronts in a huge pocket.

The German plan drafted by General Kurt Zeitzler, Chief of the OKH, was not as ambitious as the offensives of 1941 and 1942. Hitler saw it as an operation that would give Germany psychological leverage after Stalingrad and "light a bonfire" that would impress the world and possibly intimidate the Soviet high command.

It received a mixed reception from those senior officers who would be closely involved with its implementation. General Heinz Guderian, Inspector-General of Armoured

ABOVE: Red Square – the huge Stalinist development in central Kharkov seen from a Fiesler Fi156C Storch observation and liaison aircraft.

FIELD MARSHAL WALTHER MODEL

One of the more talented Field Marshals of the Third Reich, Model was born in Genthin on January 24 1891. As a young officer he published a book on the Prussian General von Gneisenau. Model served in Poland and France and commanded the 3rd Panzer Division in Russia as it drove towards the Dneiper in 1941. With his distinctive monocle and cap worn at a rakish angle, he developed a reputation as a skilled defensive fighter, earning the nickname "the Führer's Fireman". With this reputation he was posted to France in 1944 to halt the Allied breakout from Normandy. He remained a loyal and enthusiastic Nazi to the end of the war. Trapped with 325,000 German troops in the Ruhr pocket in April 1945, he shot himself in a wood near Duisburg and died on April 21 1945.

Troops, feared that the new Panther tanks were not ready for operational deployment, and that a major tank battle would deplete carefully husbanded tanks and armoured vehicles. He felt that they should be held back in anticipation of a major landing by the Allies in the West. Thinking about *Zitadelle*, he said, "made his stomach turn over".

Both Field Marshal Manstein and Colonel-General Walther Model felt that an attack on the Kursk salient was too obvious a move and would have been anticipated by the Russians. Field Marshal von Kluge, however, was in favour of launching *Zitadelle*.

Possibly the greatest triumph of ULTRA was the interception of the coded radio signals about the plans for Citadel. These were passed to the Soviet Union through the "Lucy" spy ring in Switzerland.

The spy ring was operated by a Hungarian named Sandor Rado who was assisted by Rudolf Rössler, a Bavarian journalist with strong Protestant religious convictions. Unwittingly, intelligence may also have come from Admiral Canaris, head of the *Abwehr*, the German counter-intelligence organisation, however the detailed high-grade material on the proposed Kursk offensive came from the

LEFT: Hunched low, a German soldier treads on a comrade's corpse as he makes his way down an exposed communications trench.

BELOW: Burned out T-34/76D tanks caught in an ambush in a Russian village. The open hatches suggest that the crew may have escaped.

ULTRA team at Bletchley Park.

The Lucy ring was a convenient way of filtering this information to the Soviet Union, which was not privy to the code breaking operation in Britain. Until details of the ULTRA operation became public in the 1970s, the Lucy ring was assumed to have had contacts with senior officers deep inside the OKW. ULTRA information would give the Red Army a massive advantage.

For *Unternehmen Zitadelle* the Germans brought 900,000 men, 2,700 tanks and armoured vehicles, including the Tiger and the Panther tanks, to the shoulders of the salient. They were supported by some 2,000 *Luftwaffe* fighters and bombers in the 4th and 6th *Luftflotten*. Among the aircraft that would be in action would be the unique Henschel Hs129B twin-engined ground attack fighter armed with a 7.5cm (2.9in) anti-tank gun and the Junkers Ju87G-1 with twin 3.7cm (1.4in)

ABOVE: Soldiers emerge from a farmhouse into the mud of a Russian spring that had halted the Soviet winter 1943 offensive.

ABOVE: A 2cm Flak gunner in a reversible white and field grey winter parka scans the horizon from a gun pit.

LEFT: A disabled Panther – the tank would see its combat debut at Kursk but had many unresolved development problems.

RIGHT: PzKpfw IVs loaded on flat cars are moved eastwards. The turrets are fitted with stand-off armour as a protection against shaped charge weapons.

BK (Flak 18) cannon. Besides their cannon armament, ground attack aircraft would also be carrying the new SD-1 and SD-2 bombs – these were the world's first "cluster bombs", containing respectively 180 2kg (4.4lb) or 360 1kg (2.2kg) bombs. When the SD-1 and SD-2 were dropped they opened at a pre-determined height and the smaller "bomblets" were scattered across the target area.

The cutting edge of the attack by Army Group Centre would be the 9th Army under Model, while to the south Army Group South committed the 4th *Panzerarmee* under Colonel-General Hermann Hoth with Gruppe *"Kempf"* covering its right flank.

Kursk would be the operational debut of the Panther tank. The PzKpfwV Ausf D Panther had been rushed into action from the production lines of *Maschinenfabrik* Augsburg-Nürnburg and many suffered from mechanical breakdowns and problems with their tracks. After Kursk the Soviet Army equipped whole regiments with captured Panthers and after World War II these tanks were also used by the French Army.

The disastrous armoured vehicle, the

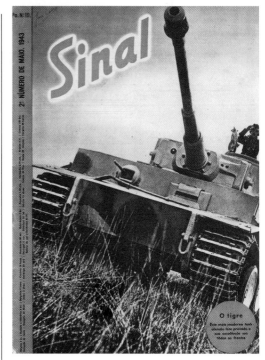

ABOVE: A spectacular *Signal* cover features the PzKpfw VI Tiger Ausf E. In action the Tiger was protected by PzKpfw IIIs or IVs that covered the vulnerable flanks.

Panzerjäger Tiger (P) *Elefant* "Elephant" SP anti-tank gun, would also go into action at Kursk for the first time. It had been the loser in the competition to design the Tiger, so the chassis that had been built were converted into huge self propelled anti-tank guns.

The attack at Kursk was first scheduled to begin on May 4 but was cancelled and reinstated for July 4 1943. Even Hitler was starting to suffer from "cold feet" and confessed that he was worried that the operation would not achieve the same level of surprise enjoyed in offensives in previous years.

He was right to be worried – to counter the attack, STAVKA, the Soviet High Command, planned to reinforce the two Fronts holding the bulge, and had deployed 13,000 guns, 6,000 anti-tank guns, 1,000 *Katyusha* multiple rocket-launchers, 3,300 tanks, 2,560 aircraft and 1,337,000 troops. Anti-tank guns, mines and infantry bunkers were grouped in armour killing grounds called *Pakfronts*.

The minefields were designed to channel the German tanks towards the anti-tank guns, and if they broke through one layer of defences there was another behind it. Soviet anti-tank mines were not as sophisticated or mechanically reliable as the German *Tellermine*. They often consisted of a demo-

KHARKOF ARMOURED ANVIL

lition charge in a waterproof box with a simple mechanism like a VPF pull or MV-5 pressure switch. The pull or load that would operate these switches could be very small and consequently they might be set off by a man. The Soviet philosophy was that if a mine virtually vaporised a soldier this would be bad for enemy morale – however, it made laying mines particularly hazardous for Soviet sappers.

In their 57mm (2.24in) M1941 anti-tank gun, however, Soviet gunners had a very powerful weapon with a muzzle velocity of 1,020 metres a second (3346ft/s) that could penetrate 140mm (5.5in) of armour at 500 metres (546yd).

The density of mines was massive: some 2,500 anti-personnel mines and 2,200 anti-tank mines per kilometre and a half of front. In all there were six belts of three to five trench lines about 50km (31 miles) deep.

GROUPE DE CHASSE 3 (GC 3), NORMANDIE-NIÉMEN

In a remarkable example of Allied collaboration, a Free French Fighter Group, Groupe de Chasse 3 (GC 3), was established in September 1942 and sent to assist the Red Air Force and travelled to the USSR via Persia. Flying Soviet Yakovlev Yak-9 fighters, it went into action in 1943 and scored its first victory when two pilots downed an Fw190 on April 5. GC 3 was in action over the Kursk battlefront in 1943 and operated in Russia until December 1944. In the 20 months its 96 pilots flew 5,240 missions and scored 273 conformed victories with 36 probables. On July 31 1944, for its part in the air battle over the River Niemen, Stalin honoured GC3 with the title "Normandy-Niémen". Among the 46 men from GC3 who were killed in action was Marcel Lefèvre who commanded the Cherbourg Squadron and who with 14 victories was the GC3's ace. He was badly burned when he was shot down on May 28 1944 and died in hospital in Moscow on June 5 1944. At a ceremony in Berlin on February 18 1953 his body was returned to the French along with those of other comrades from the group.

LEFT: By 1943 former Soviet soldiers were serving with the Wehrmacht, some out of conviction and others simply to stay alive. They wore German uniforms, but used captured Soviet weapons.

RIGHT: The crew of an SdKfz 251 washes off the whitewash camouflage with the onset of spring. The German army, though weakened, had recovered from Stalingrad and was being readied for a new offensive.

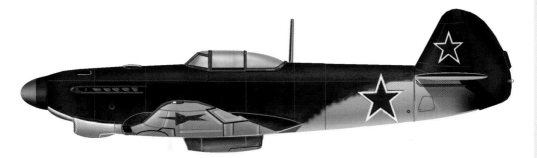

YAKOVLEV YAK-9

The Yak-9 low-level fighter and ground-attack aircraft that equipped the Free French Normandie-Niémen Regiment. One version of the Yak-9, the Yak 9-DK that had a dedicated anti-tank role, mounted a single 45mm (1.7in) NS-P-45 cannon in the nose. In the Korean War of 1950-1953 the Chinese and North Korean Air Forces used the Yak-9 in action against the USAF bombers. Total production of the Yak 9D aircraft was a staggering 16,769.

Type:	Single-engined fighter
Crew:	1
Power Plant:	1,360hp Klimov VK-105PF-3
Performance:	Maximum speed at 2,000 metres (6,560ft), 602km/h (374mph)
Range:	1,410km (876 miles)
Weights:	Empty 2,770kg (6,107lb) Loaded 3,080kg (6,790lb)
Dimensions:	Wing span 9.74m (32ft 11in) Length 8.55m (28ft) Height 3m (9ft 10in)
Armament:	One 20mm ShVAK cannon firing through the propeller hub and one12.7mm Berezin MG in the upper cowling.

GOLIATH E

The tiny Goliath E – *elektrisch* – battery-powered remote-controlled tracked demolition vehicle would have its combat debut at Kursk. The first version, designed and built by the Hansa-Lloyd-Goliath Werke Carl F. W. Borgward, was powered by two converted electric starter motors. It carried 60kg (132lb) of TNT and was directed towards its target by its operator through signals transmitted along a cable. It was 1.5m (4.9ft) long, 0.56m (1.8ft) high, 0.85m (2.7ft) wide and weighed 375kg (826.7lb). It had a road range of 1.5km (0.93 miles) and maximum speed of 10km/h (6.2mph). The Goliath V – *Vergasermotor* – was a more effective petrol-engine-powered version developed later.

ABOVE: During the build up to Kursk a company of Soviet soldiers rests in the shelter of a roadside ditch.

Marshal Zhukov and the STAVKA Chief of Staff Marshal Aleksandr Vasilevsky planned to break the impetus of the German attack and then launch Operations Kutuzov and Rumyantsev, massive counter attacks to the north and south using men and tanks held in

ABOVE: A 57mm Model 41/43 anti-tank gun. This Soviet gun that could penetrate 140mm at 500 metres remained in service after the war.

LEFT: The *Panzerjäger* Tiger (P) *Elefant*, the powerful but ill-conceived 8.8cm SP anti-tank gun that was assigned to the northern flank of the German attack at Kursk.

reserve. A complete army group, the Steppe Front under General Ivan Konev, was held in reserve either to assist the Central or Voronezh Fronts and contain the German thrusts, or to carry the counter offensive after *Zitadelle* had been stopped.

Behind the German lines partisan groups had expanded, made up of Soviet Army soldiers who had evaded capture, local men and women and political and military leaders who had been parachuted in. Ideally, partisans required a passive or friendly local population who would provide intelligence and food. Parachute drops at night would bring supplies of weapons and ammunition and others would be captured in ambushes and by theft. Dense woods, swamps or mountains were essential to provide safe areas in which the partisans could hide, train or nurse wounded.

Successful operations were undertaken

MARSHAL IVAN KONEV

Born in 1897, Ivan Stepanovich Konev, or Koniev, joined the Imperial Russian Army as a 15-year-old private. In 1918 he joined the Bolshevik Party. In the Civil War he served as a Commissar and then joined the officer corps in 1924. Konev graduated from the Frunze Military Academy in 1926. In August 1941 he served in the Smolensk sector and then from October 1941 to 1942 Konev was Commander of the Kalinin Front resisting the German advance on Moscow. In 1943 after Kursk his troops recaptured Orel, Belgorod and Poltava. From 1943-44 he commanded the Steppe Front which became the 2nd Ukrainian Front. He cut off ten German divisions at Korsun-Shevchenko, trapping about 20,000 German troops. Konev then led the 1st Ukrainian Front that took Lvov. He advanced from the Vistula to the Oder with Marshal Zhukov and occupied Berlin. He reached the Elbe and made contact with the US forces at Torgau on April 25 1945. His forces also liberated Prague. During the Soviet attack on Japanese forces in Manchuria in 1945 he was named commander of Soviet forces in the Far East Theatre. After the war he was High Commissioner for Austria and then succeeded Zhukov as Commander in Chief of Soviet ground forces and became Minister for Defence in 1955. He died in 1973.

around the cities of Yelnia and Dorogobuzh east of Smolensk, mostly conducted by Soviet Army stragglers.

Near the end of 1942 surviving elements of the Political Administration of the Soviet Army (PURKKA) brought the Army groups under central control. NKVD officers and

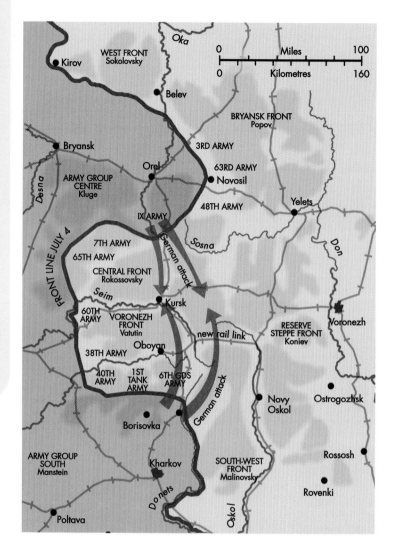

LEFT: The *Zitadelle* plan was a simple double envelopment of the Kursk salient. Unlike the attacks of 1941 and 1942 it was not an ambitious offensive into the USSR. However, even without ULTRA intelligence filtered through the Lucy spy ring, it seemed an obvious objective to STAVKA and they began to prepare for the attack.

RIGHT: The Tiger lacked the angled armour of Soviet tank designs, but its broad battle tracks gave it greater mobility across snow and mud than earlier German tanks.

RIGHT: The crew of a 10.5cm le FH 18 engage a distant target. Despite its rather archaic spoked wheels it was a modern design developed by Rheinmetall in the mid 1930s.

Komsomol members were parachuted into occupied areas to assist PURKKA. Stalin demanded that the partisans should not become a force that was not controlled by Moscow.

In 1943 the partisans began to take the war to their occupiers, concentrating on attacking road and rail links. Railways were blown up and roads mined, if the repair teams were inadequately protected they could in turn be ambushed. After Stalingrad they began to penetrate the Bryansk region and were strong around the fringes of the Pripet marshes. Other groups infiltrated the woods and swamps towards the River Dneiper and the wooded areas of the northern Ukraine.

So detailed was the Soviet knowledge of the German plan for the attack at Kursk that they launched an artillery bombardment just before the German assault was due to go in. German Freya 125MHz early warning radar however detected the Red Air Force units that

were *en route* to attack and the *Luftwaffe* intercepted the bombers and fighters. In the first moments of the battle the Russians lost 120 aircraft, by the end of the day this had risen to 432 and 24 hours later it stood at 637. In this way the Germans achieved local air superiority during the initial stages of the battle.

Though they had a tactical advantage at Kursk, the *Luftwaffe* had lost the strategic battle with the Soviet Air Force. As with tanks, once a good design had been established factories went all out to mass-produce it. In the closing months of the Stalingrad campaign the newly introduced Yakovlev Yak-9 showed that it was a tough and versatile airframe, so the huge Factory No 153 in the Urals began to build it in quantity. By the close of the war it had built 15,000 of the 30,000 Yak-9s.

UNTERNEHMEN ZITADELLE

"Soldiers of the Reich! This day you are about to take part in an offensive of such importance that the whole future of the war may depend on its outcome. More than anything else, your victory will show the whole world that resistance to the power of the German Army is hopeless."

Order of the Day for Operation Zitadelle
Adolf Hitler

O n the first day of the attack, a hot sultry afternoon on July 4, to the north the German 9th Army under Model with 900 tanks in three Panzer Corps, two Army Corps and supporting infantry, only achieved minor successes against a determined Soviet defence. They had as their objective the village of Olkhovatka about a third of the way to Kursk.

Among his forces were the *Elefant* anti-tank vehicles grouped in two battalions, *Panzerjäger* Bn653 and 654, commanded by Lt Col von Jungenfeldt. German staff were aware that the *Elefant* was vulnerable to close-range attack so infantry accompanied them riding on a sled attached by a cable to the rear of the hull. Some of the crews of *Panzerjäger* Battalion 654 commanded by

LEFT AND ABOVE: The loading and firing sequence of a 15cm *Nebelwerfer* – smoke thrower – multi-barrelled rocket launcher. It was developed at the rocket research establishment at Kummersdorf in the 1930s when Germany was banned from building heavy artillery by the Treaty of Versailles. The rocket had a 2.83kg (5.70lb) HE warhead and a maximum range of 7,060m (7,725 yards).

PZKPFW VI TIGER

Though the PzKpfw VI Tiger had none of the sloping angles of the Panther or later Tiger II, it made up for some of these design flaws by sheer strength. It entered production in August 1942 and a total of 1,350 were built before production ceased in August 1944, when it was replaced by the Tiger II. The Tiger was an excellent tank but was mechanically complex and the overlapping wheels tended to clog in snow and mud.

Armament:	8.8cm (3.4in) KwK36; one 7.92mm MG34
Armour:	25mm to 100mm (1in to 3.94in)
Crew:	5
Weight:	55,000kg (54.1 tons)
Hull length:	8.24m (27ft)
Width:	3.73m (12ft 3in)
Height:	2.86m (9ft 3in)
Engine:	Maybach HL 230 P45 12-cylinder petrol engine, 700hp
Road speed:	38km/h (24mph)
Range:	100km (62 miles)

PANZERJÄGER TIGER (P) ELEFANT

Panzerjäger Tiger (P) Elefant – "Elephant" – self-propelled anti-tank gun was armed with the powerful 8.8cm Pak 43/2/L/71 gun, but had no hull machine gun and so was incredibly vulnerable to Soviet infantry anti-tank crews. The vehicle was also known as the "Ferdinand", after its designer Ferdinand Porsche. Some Elefants were later fitted with a hull machine gun and used in a semi-static role in Italy.

Armament:	8.8cm (3.4in) KwK36
Armour:	25mm to 100mm (1in to 3.94in)
Crew:	5
Weight:	65,000kg (63.9 tons)
Hull length:	8.12m (26ft 8in)
Width:	3.37m (11ft 1in)
Height:	2.99m (9ft 10in)
Engine:	Two Maybach HL 120 TRM 12-cylinder petrol engines, 530hp
Road speed:	20.1 km/h (12.5mph)
Range:	153km (95 miles)

PzKpfw V Panther Ausf D

Very much the brainchild of Heinz Guderian, the Panther was designed to combat the T-34 that had outclassed the PzKpfw IV in Russia. MAN completed the first Panthers in September 1942. Later marks of the Panther had a hull machine gun and an AA mount by the commander's hatch. In all 5,508 Panthers were built, however production rates were initially very slow with only 12 being produced each week. The US Army estimated that it took five M4 Shermans or nine T-34s to knock out a single Panther.

Armament:	7.5cm (2.9in) KwK42; one co-axial 7.92mm MG
Armour:	30mm to 110mm (1.2in to 4.3in)
Crew:	5
Weight:	43,690kg (43 tons)
Hull length:	8.86m (29ft)
Width:	3.43m (11ft 3 in)
Height:	3.10m (10ft 2in)
Engine:	Maybach HL230 P30 700hp petrol engine
Road speed:	55 km/h (34.1mph)
Range:	177km (110 miles)

BELOW: As the axis of the southern attack diverged from the original Zitadelle plan, STAVKA was unable to second guess the Germans who began to make headway towards Prokhorovka and a massive tank battle.

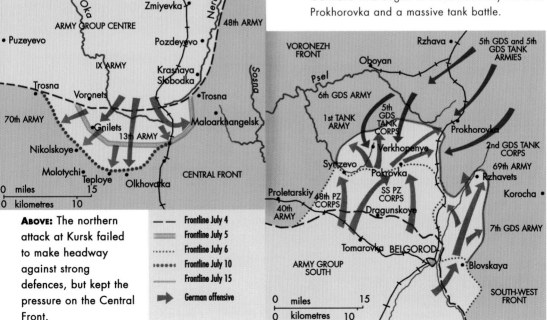

ABOVE: The northern attack at Kursk failed to make headway against strong defences, but kept the pressure on the Central Front.

Frontline July 4
Frontline July 5
Frontline July 6
Frontline July 10
Frontline July 15
German offensive

Major Noak had taken MG42 machine guns aboard their vehicles and attempted local defence by opening the breech and firing them down the 8.8cm (3.4in) barrel.

Summer rain as well as mines and anti-tank guns reduced mobility and Model's traditional use of infantry to achieve penetration for an armoured breakthrough slowed down the attacks. General Konstantin Rokossovsky, commanding the Soviet Central Front, committed his reserves, the 2nd Tank Army and a tank corps, and this forced Model into a battle of attrition. On July 7 Model switched the weight of his attack from the Orel-Kursk road towards Ponyri village to the east. Here for three days the 9th Army pounded away without result. By July 10 the Germans were on the defensive and two days later the Soviet 63rd Army and 3rd Guards Tank Army added to the pressure when they attacked towards Orel from the east and the

BELOW: A late production Tiger Ausf E with Panther-type cupola. The Tiger could cross a 1.8-metre (5ft 11in) trench and ford 1.20 metres (3ft 11in) deep water obstacles.

LEFT: The cluttered interior of a SdKfz 251 with belts of 7.92mm MG34 ammunition in the foreground and the 12-man squad of *Panzergrenadiers* hunched on the benches.

MARSHAL KONSTANTIN ROKOSSOVSKY

Born in 1896, Rokossovsky held commands in the Spanish Civil War. During the Purges of 1938 he was imprisoned but later reinstated. He commanded the Southern section of the Siberian Army during the defence of Moscow in 1941. He was then sent to Stalingrad and in December 1942 led the decisive breakthrough, cutting off the German 6th Army. In June 1944, after Kursk, he commanded the 1st Belorussian Front against the German centre and took Lublin and Brest-Litovsk but in July 1944 his advance stopped for six months just outside the Polish capital Warsaw. In August that year Polish patriots had launched an uprising in the city, but Rokossovky's armies did nothing to help. He claimed that he had insufficient supplies and was faced by strong German armoured formations. In January 1945 the Fronts were regrouped and he led the 2nd Belorussian Front which finally captured the ruined city of Warsaw. He then pushed through northern Poland, reaching the Gulf of Danzig on January 26 and trapping the German armies in East Prussia. On May 5 1945 Rokossovsky's forces linked up with the British at Lubeck. After the war he became Chief of the Armed Forces in Poland. He died in 1968.

LEFT: A shells burst close to a Soviet PTRS 1941 anti-tank rifle crew. The bolt-action rifle fired a five-round clip.

HENSCHEL Hs129B

A heavily armoured dedicated ground-attack aircraft, the Hs129 was plagued by powerplant failures throughout its operational life. It saw action in North Africa at the close of the campaign and besides Kursk was employed in Normandy in 1944. At Kursk Hs129 pilots claimed a large proportion of the Russian tanks destroyed in the fighting.

Type:	Twin-engined close-support aircraft
Crew:	1
Power Plant:	Two 700hp Gnome-Rhône 14M 4/5
Performance:	Maximum speed at 3,830m (12,570ft) 407km/h (253mph)
Range:	690km (429 miles)
Weights:	Empty 3,810kg (8,400lb)
	Maximum 5,250kg (11,574lb)
Dimensions:	Wing span 14.20m (46ft 7in)
	Length 9.75m (31ft 11in)
	Height 3.25m (10ft 8in)
Armament:	Two 7.9mm MG 17 (or two 13mm 13) machine guns in wings, two fixed forward-firing 20mm MG 151 cannon in fuselage; one (optional) 30mm MK 101 cannon in ventral pack or one 37mm (1.4in) BK 3.7; max bomb load 350kg (771lb)

JUNKERS Ju87G-1

One of the marks of the slow, but battle proven Ju87 Stuka, the anti-tank G version saw action almost exclusively in the East until the end of hostilities. It was supplied to the Rumanians and used by their air force both against Soviet ground troops and later against the Germans when Rumania switched sides.

Type:	Single-engined close-support aircraft
Crew:	2
Power Plant:	One Jumo 1,400hp Junkers Jumo 211J-1
Performance:	Maximum speed at 4,100m (13,500ft) 410km/h (255mph)
Maximum range:	1,535km (954 miles)
Weights:	Empty 3,900kg (8,600lb)
	Maximum 6,600kg (14,550lb)
Dimensions:	Wing span 13.8m (45ft 3in)
	Length 11.5m (37ft 8in)
	Height 3.88m (12ft 9in)
Armament:	Two fixed forward-firing 37mm (1.4in) BK 3.7 (Flak 18) cannon underwing, one flexible MG15 on rear cockpit.

FOCKE WULF FW190G-3

A dedicated ground-attack fighter derived from the Fw190A, the G had bomb racks fitted as standard equipment and machine guns deleted. It first saw action in Tunisia but played a significant role at Kursk. It would serve until the end of the war, including attacks at night on the Ludendorf Bridge on March 7 1945 with aircraft each carrying a single 1,800kg (3,968lb) bomb.

Type:	Long-range fighter bomber
Crew:	1
Power Plant:	One 1,700hp BMW 801D-2
Performance:	Maximum speed at sea level 573km/h (356mph)
Range:	635km (395miles)
Weights:	Empty 2,900kg (6,393lb) Loaded 4,754kg (10,480lb)
Dimensions:	Wing span 10.5m (34ft 5in) Length 8.95m (29ft 4in) Height 3.95m (12ft11in)
Armament:	Two 20mm MG 151 cannon in wings; max bomb load 1,250kg (2,755lb)

ABOVE: Tank-killer Hans-Ulrich Rudel with his Stuka rear gunner.

RIGHT: The Soviet counter attack on the northern flank of the Kursk salient. Though the Germans launched localised counter attacks the weight of tanks and artillery rolled them back remorselessly.

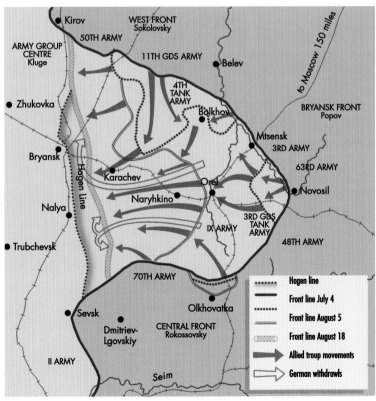

77

HANS-ULRICH RUDEL

Stuka pilot and the only recipient of the *Ritterkreuz mit goldenen Eichenlaub, Schwerten und Brillianten* – Knight's Cross with Golden Oak Leaves, Swords and Diamonds – awarded on January 1 1945. Rudel was born at Konradswaldau (Silesia) on July 2,1916. In 1937 he entered the Luftwaffe. In 1941, during the invasion of the USSR, flying a Ju87 he sunk the cruiser *Marat* in Leningrad harbour and damaged the battleship *October Revolution*. Flying the Ju87G at Kursk he was a formidable tank killer, his total confirmed kills were over 518 tanks, 700 trucks, over 150 anti-aircraft and artillery positions, nine fighter or ground-attack aircraft and hundreds of bridges, bunkers and railway lines. Rudel was shot down 32 times and in March 1944 escaped capture by Soviet troops by swimming across the 300-metre (984ft) River Dnyestr. In the spring of 1945 he was badly wounded and his right leg was partially amputated. Despite this injury he flew into Berlin in the last days of the war.

He died in Rosenheim on December 18 1982 and at his burial West German fighter pilots caused a scandal when, during a routine training mission, they flew in salute over the cemetery in the "missing man" formation.

RIGHT: Tigers roll past German soldiers with a panje wagon. Despite the arrival of new weapons and equipment the army still used horses for moving supplies and artillery, and infantry marched into action.

BELOW: The counter attacks by the Germans as they attempted to halt the massive Soviet offensive in the south. Hitler's order that troops should be withdrawn to face the Allied landings in Sicily compounded the disaster.

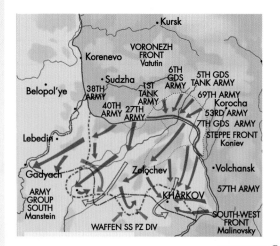

SDKFZ 165 HUMMEL

The *Hummel* or "Bumble Bee" SP gun was a hybrid of PzKpfw III and PzKpfw IV hulls. Well over 600 were built between 1942 and 1944 and the SP gun was popular with its crews, having plenty of room and 18 rounds of ready-use ammunition. Some 150 were converted to ammunition carriers, as wheeled vehicles could not keep pace with the tracked SP guns.

Armament:	One 15cm (5.9in) sIG howitzer
Armour:	20mm (max) (0.78in)
Crew:	6 - 7
Weight:	23,927kg (23.55 tons)
Hull length:	7.17m (23ft 6in)
Width:	2.87m (9ft 5in)
Height:	2.81m (9ft 2in)
Engine:	One Maybach V-12 petrol engine developing 265hp
Road speed:	42km/h (26mph)
Range:	215km (134 miles)

11th Guards Army struck deep into the 2nd *Panzerarmee* from the north. The 9th Army had lost 50,000 men, 400 tanks and 500 aircraft and shot its bolt. It was forced into a fighting withdrawal by Operation Kutuzov and fell back to the Hagen Line, a belt of fortifications in front of Bryansk.

To the south the attack by the 4th *Panzerarmee* made better headway. They had 1,500 tanks and AFVs including 94 Tigers and 200 Panthers backed by 2,500 guns and mortars. It was a formidable force made up of Hausser's II SS Panzer Corps, including the divisions *Das Reich*, *Leibstandarte* and *Totenkopf,* and Knobelsdorff's XLVIII Panzer Corps *Grossdeutschland* and *Gruppe "Kempf"* under command of Lt. General Werner Kempf.

LEFT: The crew of a T-34/76 descend from their crippled tank to surrender to a *Waffen-SS* officer.

RIGHT: A Soviet 45mm Model 1942 anti-tank gun in action. It could penetrate 95mm at 300 metres.

BELOW: Knocked out *Elefants.* The circular rear hatch was intended for the removal of the 8.8cm Pak 43/2 L/71 gun for maintenance.

Unlike the more conservative Model, Manstein and Hoth adopted a *Panzerkeil* - armoured wedge tactic. At the front of the wedge were the heavily armoured Tiger tanks and on the flanks Panthers and PzKpfw IV tanks. Behind the tanks the *Panzergrenadiers* rode into battle in SdKfz 251 half-tracks and to the rear the mortars, rocket launchers and artillery followed up. Though this was a more aggressive tactic it had one fatal flaw, the heavy armour of the Tiger and its 8.8cm (3.4in) gun equipped it to stand off from Soviet T-34/85 tanks and destroy them at long range. However when they manoeuvred within range of the T-34s and more powerful SU-85 assault guns they were vulnerable.

The T34/85 was described at the time by the Germans as "the best tank in the world". It had a crew of five and was armed with one 85mm (3in) ZIS S-53 gun with 55 rounds. The SU-85 used the proven T-34 chassis but mounted a DS-S-85 85mm (3in) gun.

The Soviet tanks were not as well finished

ABOVE: A T-34/76B, showing the large turret hatch that made the tank vulnerable to close range attack by infantry with grenades.

LEFT: A boy standing on a box operates a lathe in one of the huge Soviet armaments factories situated in the Urals.

LEFT: A Russian woman checks batches of artillery shells. The USSR was now not only producing good quality weapons, but doing so in quantity.

BELOW LEFT: A column of German 7.5cm StuG III assault guns. Cheaper and faster to build, assault guns were a poor substitute for tanks.

BELOW: A cigarette shared by an infantry officer who wears tank destruction badges and a German PzKpfw IV tank crew.

as German or Allied vehicles, the welded finish looked crude and the interiors were not as comfortable. They were however reliable and rugged, despite being mass produced. Early in the war the Soviet munitions industry had been evacuated from the western borders and moved thousands of miles to the east. At a chain of factories in cities beyond the Ural Mountains at Nizhni Tagill, Sverdlovsk, Omsk and the huge "Tankograd" plant at Chelyabinsk, men and women worked in grim conditions to produce tanks by the thousand.

The Soviet artillery arm was not only powerful, but it, too, was used in mass. Huge barrages would crash down on enemy assembly areas or advancing forces and precede the Soviet counter attacks. The principal weapons were the 122mm (4.8in) M 1939 and the 152mm (5.9in) M1937 howitzer.

The M1939 howitzer had a crew of eight, and fired 21.8kg (48lb) HE shell to a maximum range of 11,800 metres (7.3 miles). An experienced and fully manned crew could fire five to six rounds a minute.

The M1937 howitzer weighed 7,128kg (7 tons) in action and fired a 43.6kg (96lb) shell to maximum range of 17,265m (10.7 miles). A trained crew could keep up a rate of fire of four rounds a minute. From 1943 onwards the gun was also mounted on the JSU-152 heavy assault gun and used against tanks and rein-

FAR LEFT: Using crude but effective tactics, Soviet infantry armed with PpSh submachine guns advance under fire behind T-34/76D tanks.

ABOVE: A *Waffen-SS* 8.1cm mortar crew manpack its weapon past armoured vehicles in the standing crops of the Kursk salient.

LEFT: The crew of a T-34/76 bales out from its blazing vehicle. Ammunition inside a burning tank would quickly explode.

forced concrete emplacements.

In addition to artillery, the Soviet forces had US-supplied 6 x 4 Studebaker $2^1/_2$-ton trucks fitted with M13 16-rail launchers for 132mm (5.1in) Katyusha – Little Katy rockets. Known to German soldiers as "Stalin's Organ" because of the distinctive howl from the rocket, they had an awesome blast effect when a salvo of 16 rockets hit a target.

An idea of the effect of a massed bombardment is given in a description by the Soviet war correspondent Yvgeny Vorobyev: "The air shook from the guns firing in salvos. All kept their mouths open, looking like stunned fish landed on shore. And all were stunned indeed, because by its nature the human ear cannot endure so much infernal din, roar and clang...

"In the south the horizon disappeared behind a screen of smoke and earth. Kicked up by shell bursts the black mass of earth remained hanging in mid air in defiance of the law of gravity. Before the particles of earth thrown up from shell craters could settle, they were propelled upwards by new blasts and lumps of kicked-up earth."

ABOVE: A PzKpfw III Ausf J, with extra armour skirts covering the turret and tracks, in a loose formation on the steppe. This formation made tanks less vulnerable to artillery fire.

RIGHT: Armoured warfare in Russia – the distant horizon with vehicles and black rising smoke from knocked out tanks.

On July 4 probes by Ott's LII Corps and Knobelsdorff's Panzer Corps directly to the south of Oboyan pushed back General Chistyakov's 6th Guards Army. Rain and heavy Soviet artillery fire slowed down the attacks.

The next day at 05.00 hours the German attack was resumed by the XLVIII and II SS-Panzer Corps. By nightfall both corps appeared to be through the Soviet defences, however, as their lines were breached, the Soviet forces fell back to pre-prepared positions.

Manstein and Hoth realised that they would not achieve a link up with the 9th Army attacking north towards Oboyan and assessed that the Soviet forces would attempt a counter attack from the direction of Prokhorovka.

They planned to halt this attack before driving north again. Now that German generals were thinking on their feet and not working a plan that was known to STAVKA events were beginning to run in their favour.

On July 6 the 4th *Panzerarmee* continued its thrusts towards Oboyan, but they were now encountering Lt. Gen M.Y.Katukov's 1st Tank Army dug in behind the 6th Guards Army. The General had with him a formidable political officer in Nikita Khruschev. Khruschev had already provided the backbone to the hard-pressed 62nd Army at Stalingrad. At Kursk the duration of the fighting would be shorter, but very intense.

Hauser's II SS-Panzer Corps had by now advanced 40km (25 miles) into Chistakov's front. The *Waffen-SS* troops kept up the pressure and by July 7 the situation began to look critical for the Voronezh Front. The Soviet forces, however, had the benefit of interior lines and with the threat in the north neutralised were able to transfer more artillery and General Rodmistrov's 5th Guards Tank Army and General Zhadov's 5th Guards Tank Army from the Steppe Front.

The summer sun had dried out the steppe by July 8 and individual German formations were making slow, but effective progress. However, by now Hoth's forces had been in action for five days and fuel and ammunition were beginning to run low. They had punched a roughly rectangular salient into the Voronezh Front, about 18km (11.2 miles) deep and 30km (18.6 miles) wide. However, two days later, after establishing a bridgehead on the River Psel and pushing towards Oboyan, the 4th *Panzerarmee* was about 40km (24.8 miles) into the Soviet lines.

To the north of the Kursk salient Model had been forced onto the defensive and this took pressure off STAVKA.

On July 12 the II *SS-Panzer Corps* had broken through the last Soviet defence line,

ABOVE: Red Air Force armourers prepare bombs for a camouflaged Petlyakov Pe-2 dive bomber which had a 1,200kg bomb load.

TOP RIGHT: German infantry in training for close combat action against tanks hunch low as one drives across them.

RIGHT: Soviet soldiers examine a captured PzKpfw IV Ausf F2. Spare tracks have been added to protect the hull and glacis plate.

reaching the village of Prokhorovka. It was here that it encountered the tanks and assault guns of the 5th Guards Tank Army. In the ensuing maelstrom of dust, smoke and flame about 572 tanks and AFVs, three quarters of

ABOVE: Spoils of war: a knocked-out StuG III Ausf G. The commander had an MG34 protected by an armoured shield.

BELOW: A smashed PzKpfw IV Ausf G with the long 7.5cm gun.

them Soviet, fought a tank battle that the Soviet Union reported as the largest in history. Dust and smoke obscured the sky and this hindered air operations by both sides.

The Allied landings on Sicily on July 10 prompted Hitler to order a halt to *Zitadelle*.

He insisted that the 2nd SS-Panzer Corps, which he rated as the equivalent of 20 Italian divisions, should be withdrawn and sent south to Italy to halt the landings.

Manstein, however, believed that the Soviet reserves were running out and that if Model could keep the pressure on the northern flank he would achieve a break in. It is one of the great "what ifs" of Kursk whether it would have been a German victory if Manstein had been allowed to keep up his attacks. The Voronezh Front had been obliged to call on the Steppe Front to contain the attacks and despite heavy rain Manstein's forces had trapped the Soviet 69th Army and two tank corps between Rzhavets, Belenikhino and Gostishchevo. Since the beginning of the operation his forces had

taken 24,000 prisoners, destroyed or captured 1,000 tanks and over 100 anti-tank guns.

On July 13 Manstein and Kluge were summoned to the *Wolfsschanze* – the Wolf's Lair HQ in Rastenburg, East Prussia. Hitler said they were to break off *Zitadelle* and direct troops to Western Europe to contain the Allies. Pressed by Manstein, Hitler agreed that Hoth and Kempf could continue their attacks in the south, but that Model should give up forces.

The strategic balance was changing, not only in the Mediterranean, but also with the opening of the Soviet counter offensives. To the south, Operation Rumyantsev', the attack by the Voronezh Front and Steppe Front, was launched on August 3. The 40th and 27th Armies to the north and 57th Army from the

LEFT: A column of German PoWs waits to be marched to the rear. With some justification the Soviet Union kept its prisoners longer than the West, using some of them for reconstruction tasks until the early 1950s. The loss of experienced soldiers put a severe strain on German manpower from 1943 and increasingly former Soviet PoWs were used in the West to man positions on the Atlantic Wall.

BLITZKRIEG

ABOVE: A park of captured German tanks, including a PzKpfw IV Ausf F, is inspected by Soviet officers. On the Eastern Front both sides employed captured vehicles and weapons.

RIGHT: Ripped apart from the explosion of its on-board ammunition, the wreck of one of many German tanks that littered the Kursk battlefield.

South West Front to the east, launched attacks on the shoulder of the German salient.

The 4th *Panzer Armee* and *Gruppe "Kempf"* fought a hard action as they withdrew, counter attacking on August 11–17 against the Voronezh Front south of Bogudukhov and delaying the Soviet advance, but not halting it. By the end of the fighting each side had lost about 1,500 tanks, but many of the Soviet ones could be recovered and repaired.

On the northern shoulder of the Kursk salient General Nikolai Pukhov, commanding the Soviet 13th Army, surveyed the battlefield. "Everywhere were signs of recent fighting. The entire expanse had been ploughed up by artillery and mortar shells and bombs. Everywhere were deep craters, tangles of

barbed wire, cut down or broken trees. The grass and crops had been stomped into the ground by thousands of feet.

"Chimneys were all that was left of the villages burnt down by the retreating Nazis. Everything was broken, crushed. Only a distant hillock somehow left untouched by artillery shells would sometimes bristle with crosses over countless German graves. The enemy paid with thousands of such graves for his attempt to topple us on the Kursk bulge…"

On August 13 Soviet forces reached the outskirts of Kharkov and German forces were forced to withdraw to avoid encirclement. The city was liberated on August 23. It was shell-gutted, burned and blasted. In the days that followed, Soviet engineers working patiently in the dirt and rubble removed 61,000 mines and 320 aircraft bombs rigged as mines.

Now across most of the USSR the Soviet Fronts were on the offensive. Many men thought that they had a secure line to fall back to in the misleadingly named East Wall or Panther Line. These defences based on the river Dniepr were anchored in the south on the Sea of Azov and in the north on Lake Peipus and the Gulf of Leningrad.

The Germans were back in position by late September, but because of their huge casualties and the poor siting of some of the defences they were in no position to hold the East Wall.

The Soviet Army was now a more mobile and flexible force and the OKW knew that after the winter had hardened the mud the German forces in the East would be faced by a new offensive.

LEFT: Soviet tank crews look at the hits on a Tiger turret from solid shot. Weapons were sometimes tested at different ranges against captured tanks, however this one is probably the victim of the tough close-range action at Prokhorovka.

BLITZKRIEG

INDEX

LEFT: An exhausted and despairing German NCO sits on the trail of a smashed 10.5cm sIG 33 infantry gun, one of the oldest weapons in service in the German Army.

INDEX